FIVE KEYS
TO POWERFUL
BUSINESS
RELATIONSHIPS

How to Become More Productive, Effective, and Influential

SALLIE J. SHERMAN
JOSEPH P. SPERRY
STEVE VUCELICH

Mc
Graw
Hill
Education

New York   Chicago   San Francisco   Athens   London   Madrid
Mexico City   Milan   New Delhi   Singapore   Sydney   Toronto

1 2 3 4 5 6 7 8 9   DOC/DOC   1 0 9 8 7 6 5 4 3

ISBN   978-0-07-178388-0
MHID   0-07-178388-1

e-ISBN 978-0-07-178389-7
e-MHID   0-07-178389-X

Library of Congress Cataloging-in-Publication Data

Sherman, Sallie.
    Five keys to powerful business relationships : how to become more
  productive, effective and influential / by Sallie J. Sherman, Joseph P. Sperry,
  and Steve Vucelich.
      pages cm
    Includes bibliographical references.
    ISBN-13: 978-0-07-178388-0 (alk. paper)
    ISBN-10: 0-07-178388-1 (alk. paper)
    1. Business networks. 2. Strategic alliances (Business) 3. Executive ability.
  4. Interpersonal relations. I. Sperry, Joseph. II. Vucelich, Steve. III. Title.
  HD69.S8S536 2014
  650.1'3--dc23   2013014380

McGraw-Hill Education books are available at special quantity discounts to use as premiums and sales promotions or for use in corporate training programs. To contact a representative, please visit the Contact Us page at www.mhprofessional.com.

Contents

V
ery simply, this book is about unleashing the power of business relationships to help you, your company, and your various stakeholders grow and thrive. As business relationship experts for almost three decades, these authors have served as trusted advisors to senior leadership across a host of industries around the globe. I'm delighted they have chosen to share with a broader audience a set of practices derived from their work with hundreds of clients and thousands of business relationships.

I've had the good fortune to work closely with S4 Consulting and the authors of this book in several contexts over the past 15 years. I find their approach unique, refreshing, and most important, immensely effective. *Five Keys to Powerful Business Relationships* goes beyond the usual bonhomie, grip-and-grin, back-slapping, going-to-the-ballgame, sending-birthday-cards dimension of business relationships. This book outlines a fresh, more systematic perspective to an area usually thought of as the "soft" side of business acumen. Indeed, managing business relationships as assets is a blend of science and art that can provide tremendous economic value.

This book is foundational. Powerful business relationships—internally and externally—are critically important to efficiently, effectively, and profitably executing any corporate or organizational mission. This is becoming increasingly important as our economy and business arrangements become more collaborative and interdependent.

This book even applies its keys to digital and virtual business relationships. The timing is right for this book in the world of exploding social media and social networks in a global economy. In a world of networked Facebook "friends" and LinkedIn "connections," we all have perhaps more acquaintances than ever before. This book provides tactics to transform a breadth of connections into deep relationships that get work done. Social networks have tremendous potential power, and the Five Keys can help you to realize and activate their potential.

This book is practical and written to benefit the reader by making the Five Keys easy to understand and implement. The book captures the voices, stories, and examples of those who have successfully built, managed, and benefited from powerful business relationships in a variety of contexts—small businesses, Fortune 100 firms, government, nonprofits, educational institutions, the military, startups, service companies, and manufacturing organizations.

Five Keys to Powerful Business Relationships is a valuable book for those of us who are involved in the day-to-day reality of business and organizational relationships. In fact, "those of us" is pretty much all of us. Nearly everyone interacts with other people in a variety of settings, and all can benefit from the Five Keys.

I hope that you enjoy and benefit from this book. Perhaps more important, I hope that those with whom you have a business relationship also will benefit from your investment in the *Five Keys to Powerful Business Relationships*. Put the Five Keys to work in your life to grow and thrive.

Bradley J. Mitchell
Chief Commercial Officer
AccuWeather
State College, PA
December 2012

Acknowledgments

There are so many people who have inspired and helped us with this book that it is hard to know where to begin thanking people. All those with whom we have worked over the years have, in some way, contributed to this book. To all of you, we are deeply grateful for your support. Thank you.

Some people have made direct contributions to this book. First, we are deeply indebted to those of you who so graciously shared your time and expertise to be interviewed for this work. We hope that you learned from and enjoyed the experience as much as we did. These include Bruce Barnes, Domonic Biggi, Tom Feeney, Peter Goldsmith, Jim Hallett, Joan Holmes, Jerry Hultin, Paula Marshall, Angelo Mazzocco, Doug Renfro, Jeff Schwantz, Derek Smith, James Thomas, and Nicholas Wolfson.

Second, there are the trusted partners and colleagues who for years have worked with us not only to study and train but also to masterfully practice and promote fostering healthy business relationships. You have helped us to evolve and refine our thinking—and the quality of all our relationships: So thank you Jose Acevedo, Jack Fish, Belinda Gore, Jim Guilkey, Erin Hinkle, Kathy Hoyt, Jill Hultin, Dave Jones, Wes Mayer, Dan Shaffer, Sally Trethewey, Art van Bodegraven, Kim Wilson, and Nicholas Wolfson.

Third, thank you to the clients and associates whom we admire and respect because you lead your companies or areas based on the keys discussed in this book. You know who you are. You have been a blessing to us. You have shared our passion, lightened our load, and made our work more rewarding. We hope that we have done the same for you.

Fourth, we'd like to acknowledge and thank those of you who directly contributed to the writing of this book. We could not have done it without you! Our thanks go to Jose Acevedo, Belinda Gore, Kim Haaf, Erin Hinkle, Mimi Kuehn, Thom McCain, Brad Mitchell, Tom Owens, Matt Russo, Dan Shaffer, Megha Tikoo, Sally Trethewey, Kim Wilson, and Nicholas Wolfson. Our special thanks go to Knox Houston, senior editor at McGraw-Hill, who has believed in us and walked with us on this journey.

Finally, we thank our families and friends who supported and loved us even when we weren't always at our best. You have taught us the most about what it means to live each day in a healthy and powerful relationship. We love you all.

To all these and countless others of you who have made us better because of our relationships with you, we thank you!

Sallie, Joe, and Steve

PART 1

Introduction and Overview of the Five Keys

Wondering what you need to do to be more productive, effective and influential? Wondering why you are a hard worker and have good technical skills but are not being appreciated? The five keys can open some new doors for you.

Why This Book?

This book is meant to encourage and guide businesspeople who want to become more productive, effective, and influential. We know how powerful it can be to transform critical business relationships. For almost three decades, we've helped business leaders and their companies develop and nurture powerful relationships that, in turn, have enabled them, their people, and their businesses to grow and thrive. Over the years we have found again and again that the fastest-growing businesses focus not simply on strategic planning or dollars. They also systematically focus on unleashing the power of their business relationships—between individuals; among teams and divisions; and with suppliers, customers, and strategic partners.

In our early days of working together, we sought to understand what businesses could do to have the greatest impact on economic value. Our work in product and service quality and their impact on customer satisfaction kept taking us back to the importance of relationships—and their value as corporate assets. At one time there was not much interest in or appetite for unleashing the power of business relationships. Because advertising was seen as the solution to most customer-acquisition challenges, the mantra was, "If you build a product, they [customers] will come." This certainly worked for a while, but the increasingly global economy, quality movement, rapid increase in mergers/acquisitions, quickly evolving technology, and outsourcing soon changed the heavy reliance on advertising. Paradoxically, in an increasingly high-tech world, the need for and importance of strong business relationships has increased dramatically. Today, in an era of greater collaboration and strategic partnerships, business leaders are spending countless hours and resources trying to maximize their human capital and strategic business relationships. We've come a long way.

Along this journey, we've worked with a great many business-people, some of them very technically competent businesspeople, who have been frustrated by their lack of recognition and/or pro-motions. They asked, "If I have good technical skills and do great work, why am I not getting ahead? Why are those whom I perceive as less competent passing me by? Why am I stuck?" This book was written to answer those questions and others.

For too long we've watched these businesspeople struggle with their lack of personal power and inability to develop and nurture strong, healthy business relationships. We have been saddened by their struggle. It doesn't have to be that hard. By understanding the practices that relationship masters use, you can experiment with these approaches and see which work best for you. Of one thing we're sure: *There is no one "right way" to develop relationships.* Some things generally work better than others, but we have seen things that we never thought would work, work powerfully. In the late 1980s, when we were helping with the divestiture of the Bell Systems and the emergence of AT&T, we got to see firsthand what happened when relationships were broken, restored, or recreated. Anyone who worked in the phone companies through that era knows what we mean. Working with very technical and world-renowned areas of the company, we got to see firsthand how helping scientists more effectively relate with their colleagues and customers increased their effectiveness and personal power. Some technical experts acknowledged that they were not particularly effective in person-to-person interactions and that it had never occurred to them that there might be practices they could use to be more successful in those situations. They also admitted that they never realized that their lack of relationship skills—skills they saw as "soft," inauthentic, or unnecessary—might be holding them back in their careers or keeping them from the recognition they so richly deserved.

Over the next three decades, we found ourselves working with hundreds of companies, from information technology (IT) firms to highly regulated companies in energy, gas, transportation, pharmaceuticals, and financial services. In each of these, we have worked with people at all levels and in all functions to develop or transform their business relationships so as to help them and their companies grow and thrive. Along the way, we have been asked to write up our approaches so that others in the firms could develop their skills. This was our primary impetus for writing *Five Keys to Powerful Business Relationships*.

In our successful first book, *The Seven Keys to Managing Strategic Accounts* (McGraw-Hill, 2003), we focused more on large business-to-business relationships. We presented business cases to demonstrate how suppliers using a relationship-management strategy, paired with appropriate infrastructure and organizational alignment, can achieve extraordinary bottom-line results. In *Five Keys to Powerful Business Relationships* we will be showing how to unleash the power in both the internal and external relationships that drive performance.

What This Book Is Not

This book is not

>> Twenty-five easy tips to better business relationships in 25 days
>> *The* Five Keys to Powerful Business Relationships
>> A textbook nor a treatise studying hundreds of companies

As we said, this book is not "twenty-five easy tips for better business relationships in 25 days." Sorry, that's just not us. Relationships are too complicated and interwoven. Think of a Rubik's Cube. All the small blocks are connected to all the other small blocks. Move one cube column and things can change dramatically. There are over 40,000 possible ways to move the individual pieces, and we know that in attempting to solve one of these cubes, we've tried at least 36,000 moves. It takes patience and practice to solve the cube. There are similar complexities to relationships. An approach, for example, used successfully with one relationship may not necessarily work with another person in the same situation. To even think that relationships could be handled with "easy tips" does not recognize their inherent complexity. Instead of tips, we will be sharing with you *practices of successful businesspeople*—primarily executives—whom we and others have identified as very effective relationship builders and developers.

The book is also <u>not</u> *The* Five Keys to Powerful Business Relationships. We have selected practices we know are successful in developing and maintaining effective relationships. We would be the last to suggest that these are somehow comprehensive choices. All these keys are interconnected, though, and can be enormously effective when used together.

Finally, this book is neither a textbook nor a treatise studying hundreds of companies. We cite some of those studies, but our interest here is not academic; we wrote this book to help you learn from and experiment with successful practices we and others have identified so that you too can create more powerful relationships to grow and thrive. We've written this book to help you along your relationship-development journey.

Lessons from People Nominated as Relationship Masters

When we decided to write this book, we asked a number of colleagues and clients to nominate people they knew who were master relationship builders. A gratifying number of those nominated agreed to be interviewed so that we could share some of the practices that have made them so successful.

There are also many with whom we have worked who are masterful relationship builders who are not specifically named in this book. For that we apologize. Please keep doing what you're doing and know that we're still your biggest fans.

An Overview of the Five Keys to Powerful Business Relationships

We are all long-time business readers. We know that few businesspeople read straight through a book. Instead, they look for the chapters they think apply to them most directly and start there. The five keys, though, are closely interrelated and affect one another. Each relationship key can, and will, help you to build powerful business relationships on its own. To help you decide where to begin, here is an overview:

Why Care about Powerful Business Relationships?
Key #1: Connect First; Then Focus on Task
Key #2: Learn by Walking in Another's Shoes
Key #3: Whether People Trust You Is Often up to You
Key #4: Share Information to Increase Your Personal Power
Key #5: Manage Yourself before You Manage Others
A Review of the Five Keys
Virtual Relationships and the Five Keys
For Leaders: Three Relationship Challenges

Why Care about Powerful Business Relationships?

This chapter lays the groundwork for the rest of the book. Before you invest in developing powerful business relationships or encouraging others to do so, you need to fully understand why doing so makes business sense. We talk about why you should care and what we mean when we think about business relationships, and we use Southwest Airlines as an example of a firm that values and receives value from what it calls "relational competence."[1] We then present five successful practices that we have seen used by the best relationship managers we know, and we define and link relationship power, personal energy, and firm productivity. The book's overall goal is to help you, as a businessperson, to see and develop the power of relationships.

We believe that almost any business can strengthen critical relationships inside and outside the firm. The process starts, though, with people understanding the power of relationships.

Key #1: Connect First; Then Focus on Task

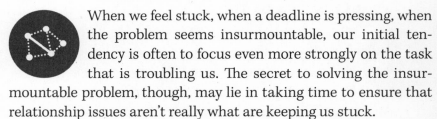 When we feel stuck, when a deadline is pressing, when the problem seems insurmountable, our initial tendency is often to focus even more strongly on the task that is troubling us. The secret to solving the insurmountable problem, though, may lie in taking time to ensure that relationship issues aren't really what are keeping us stuck.

In Key #1 we will be speaking about how to unstick people in problem-solving team meetings where everyone initially wants to focus entirely on task. Such a task focus too often results in less than optimal solutions.

Key #2: Learn by Walking in Another's Shoes

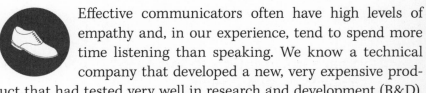 Effective communicators often have high levels of empathy and, in our experience, tend to spend more time listening than speaking. We know a technical company that developed a new, very expensive product that had tested very well in research and development (R&D). The problem was that the product had been designed more for technical elegance than for customer usage. The product, for example, had some portability but needed a great deal more if it was going to be adopted by many health-care customers. The designers had lacked a clear sense of the customers' expectations, how the product would be used, and how often and where it was going to be moved. In this case, these questions had to be asked after

the product had come out, and unfortunately, retooling products is usually much more expensive than getting them right the first time.

In Key #2 we'll talk about examples of business issues that hinge on certain kinds of empathy—knowing someone's expectations, needs, and wishes—and the impact this can make on business results.

Key #3: Whether People Trust You Is Often up to You

 Trust is a concept that appears simple but is actually made up of many dimensions and contexts. Among other things, it involves the intentions of the person to be trusted, his or her actions, and how closely aligned are his or her words and actions. Throw in the fact that some people are inherently trusting and others inherently distrustful and you have enough variables to make trust a concept as slippery as a freshly caught fish.

Because trust can be one of the major causes of relationship problems, Key #3 focuses on some of its dimensions, allowing managers to see what may be missing in their own sense of trust, how long it takes them to develop trust, and the practices they can use to develop that trust.

Key #4: Share Information to Increase Your Personal Power

 In an older business model, people tended to see knowledge as power; the more they hoarded information, the more powerful they were. Department managers were sometimes less than forthcoming to other functional areas. In newer business models, such a notion is turned on its head. In many cases, sharing knowledge and building relationships now make you *more* powerful. By letting people know what you know, you give them options to create better decisions, tactics, and strategies. Sharing information, in our experience, is one of the keys to creating innovative solutions and increasing your personal power.

In one heavily engineering-based company, people hoarded knowledge, except for one executive. This executive proactively shared information and freely answered questions. Colleagues eagerly sought his advice and guidance. In turn, this sharing empowered the executive's team, and the more powerful they became, the better their results were.

Key #5: Manage Yourself before You Manage Others

We tend to see ourselves as rational people, but there are parts of us that are irrational. We have fears, dreams, and hopes that can keep us from being our most successful. How many great ideas stay buried because employees are afraid to look foolish in front of their peers or their bosses? Only recently have brain scientists helped us to understand the function of the amygdala, the part of the brain that continually scans our environment for perceived danger and works to keep us safe. How does this brain area link to building relationships? When we are under stress, our amygdala can send messages so loud and demanding that it causes us to listen more to our own fears than to the other people with whom we are working, perhaps undermining our relationships and effectiveness.

Key #5 looks at self-knowledge—perhaps the most critical kind of knowledge—as a foundation to your managerial and personal effectiveness. Without self-knowledge, our business efforts may be for naught. Without self-knowledge, we may be blind and ineffective because we may be unaware of our impact on others. Better understanding of ourselves allows us to be better listeners, problem solvers, colleagues, and customers (and lovers). It enables us to communicate more clearly and more effectively. It allows us to influence without authority, unleashing our personal power.

A Review of the Five Keys

This chapter will summarize our five keys, provide some checklists for developing and maintaining those practices, and present the sources we have found invaluable in learning about relationship competence. The goal is to help people to take the next step in more effectively managing themselves and their critical business relationships. Building powerful business relationships is a challenging yet fulfilling journey. Our role is to help make that journey easier.

Virtual Relationships and the Five Keys

We felt that we needed to explore virtual relationships because the vast majority of businesspeople have them, and there are some specific challenges to connections through communications platforms. A great many people assume that if a message is clear to them, it will be clear to other people. In our experience, this assumption is often incorrect. Thus, if the recipient receives the message and it is a note that is hard to read or, heaven forbid, perceived as being sarcastic, there can easily be hell to pay. We speak from painful experience.

For Leaders: Three Relationship Challenges

In this final chapter we examine three particular challenges a leader faces: (1) the challenges of staying true to yourself—maintaining authenticity; (2) the challenge of managing multiple relationships—why you probably should not have 26,000 people in your contact list; and (3) the challenge of installing a culture that promotes healthy empowering relationships. We've heard from a number of businesspeople who have faced all three challenges—and overcame them.

PART 2

Why Care about Powerful Business Relationships?

Power in organizations is the capacity generated by relationships.

—MARGARET J. WHEATLEY[1]

Like you, we often have learned the hard way. We've gone to meetings focused on efficiently completing a task, only to have the meeting derailed by some unexpected relationship issue. Or we've said something meant to be supportive, only to be totally misunderstood. Or we've been involved in a seemingly straightforward project, only to watch it become so frustrating and painful because of team dynamics that it hardly seemed worth the effort. It has never ceased to amaze us how much business relationships affect business outcomes.

For almost three decades we have been helping businesses become more competitive and profitable. Originally we thought product and service quality were the keys to success, but we soon learned that in many cases it was the quality of business relationships that profoundly affected business results. Since that time, our primary focus has been on strengthening key relationships—within teams, among departments, with suppliers, and with customers. We have seen that by focusing on developing powerful, empowering business relationships, we have a fulcrum on which to lever our clients to better business performance. We work, in other words, to harness the power that Wheatley defines in this chapter's opening epigraph.

What Are Powerful Business Relationships?

For us, powerful business relationships bring out the best in all parties. They let us be who we are at work without us having to worry about being politically correct and/or inauthentic. When we define these relationships, we are not speaking about manipulating or suppressing others. We believe instead that the most powerful business relationships are built on influence instead of control, openness instead of suppression. These sorts of relationships lie at the heart of collaboration and both value and engage us. We see them constantly improving the performance of individuals, teams, and companies. That is so because these relationships create environments in which people and businesses can grow and thrive.

Benefits for You

Powerful business relationships

>> Bring out your best and the best of those around you
>> Make your work more efficient, productive, and meaningful
>> Enhance performance
>> Increase your influence and prestige
>> Make your work and life easier and *a great deal* more fun
>> Allow you and others to grow and thrive

What Happens When Business Relationships Don't Work?

Think of a functioning business as a hose through which water (productivity) flows. Now think of a dysfunctional business relationship as a crimp in that hose. Even in the smallest firms, there are a great many crimped hoses, all of which reduce business

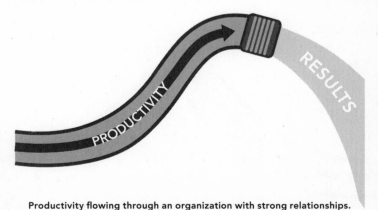

Productivity flowing through an organization with strong relationships.

results. If you are an executive, you know how very difficult it is to capture the positive effects from good relationships. Our experience has revealed, however, that most executives, managers, and staff usually have some idea as to how much "crimped hoses"—ineffective relationships—have cost them, at least in irritation, lost time, and occasionally even hard dollars. For example,

>> How many product launches have been missed because of ineffective team relationships and skewed communication, perhaps owing to a lack of trust or different working styles?
>> How many critical reports have arrived late because managers or departments were warring over the "right" way to present information (i.e., the best way to shine their function's contribution)?
>> How many teams fail because there are powerful subgroups that refuse to share information with each other?
>> How many teams go under because one of the members has a pocket veto for decisions she does not agree with?

Our experience has been that when business relationships work well, they unleash power for employees and firms. This unleashing can allow you to leverage superior results and achieve exponential returns and a competitive advantage. When those same relationships don't work, your firm may be moving forward, but these dysfunctional relationships act like anchors keeping it from achieving top speed.

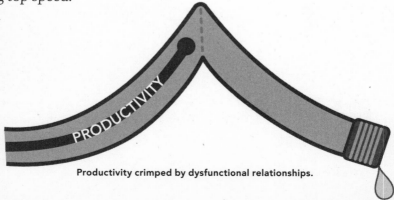

Productivity crimped by dysfunctional relationships.

Let's talk about the potential anchors in one relationship we all know: the doctor-patient relationship. In this relationship, great technical skills, applied without relational competence, can dramatically crimp the hose, leading to misdiagnosis and high-dollar malpractice lawsuits. Over the last 15 years, a number

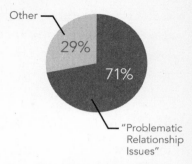

Reasons given for medical malpractice suits.

of studies have examined the top reasons doctors are sued for malpractice. In one study where the authors looked over plaintiff legal depositions to determine the reasons for lawsuits, they found that patients who have sued for malpractice are likely to have "problematic relationship issues" with their doctor (71 percent). The four main relationship problems patients gave for suing are (1) deserting the patient (not being accessible; 32 percent), (2) devaluing patient and/or family views (29 percent), (3) delivering information poorly (26 percent), and (4) failing to understand the patient and/or family perspective (13 percent).[2] Each malpractice suit was for hundreds of thousands of dollars.

If you'd like to hear more about the financial impact of those settlements on physicians, ask a doctor friend about what his

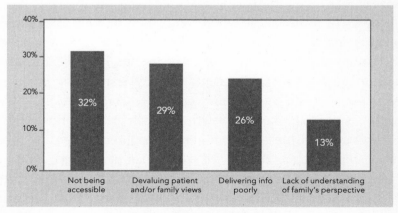

Problematic Relationship Issues

malpractice insurance now costs compared with last year or five years ago. After you ask the question, we would suggest that you take a step back and ready yourself for the venting that is almost certain to occur.

Why Have Relationships Been Undervalued?

If the only thing preventing doctors from being sued and teams from missing critical deadlines is a lack of quality relationships, why aren't people and businesses spending more time on developing the skills needed to develop them?

We find that very few businesspeople disagree with us when we say that relationships ought to be treated as assets and that how those assets are treated goes a long way toward explaining firm success. If there is such high agreement about the importance of relationships, though, why is business so full of dysfunctional ones?

Dysfunctional relationships often exist because many of us have not developed our business relationship *skills*. We may understand the concepts in theory but have not had the necessary practice. Many firms also have cultures that value technical skill development and short-term dollars over long-term relationship skill development. These firms see social skills as somehow "soft" and unworthy of investment. Why spend money on intangible skills whose results cannot be easily measured?

Why do firms see these relationship skills as soft? The primary reason is that it's virtually impossible to run a traditional cost-justification analysis for effective relationships. Because it is much easier to cost justify investments on physical assets, firms—in many cases—spend more money on servers, buildings, and other tangible assets than they do investing in their critical employee and customer relationships. This is especially frightening because those relationships (such as those with strategic or global accounts) can be thousands of times more valuable than the firm's physical assets.

Businesspeople—MBAs, boards of directors, and executive teams—are taught that if you cannot justify it financially, *you should not make the investment.* This is why relationships, whose values are almost always nonquantifiable, are seen as soft. Too many firms are wary of investing in people and relationship skills. For many companies, investments in developing relationship skills are too often put on the back burner or never even make it onto the stovetop, and then those same firms may wonder why their people are underperforming.

W. Edwards Deming is best known for his early insights into achieving product quality through statistical control. In his best-known book, *Out of the Crisis,* 99 percent of what he says deals with creating systems and processes to achieve consistent product quality. But, although it's often ignored, Deming also says some very insightful things about service and relationship quality.

At one point he argues that ignoring the "soft stuff" can undermine any firm's effectiveness. Deming recognizes the weakness of traditional bookkeeping, saying that management "cannot be successful [managing] on visible figures alone. . . . he that would run his company on visible figures alone will in time have neither company nor figures."[3] By "visible figures," Deming is speaking about the numbers generated by traditional cost accounting. Deming says that "the most important figures that one needs for management are unknown or unknowable, but successful management must nevertheless take account of them."[4]

What sorts of invisible figures are crucial? As Deming says, "Examples: The multiplying effect on sales that comes from a happy customer, and the opposite effect from an unhappy customer. The happy customer that comes back for more is worth ten prospects. He comes without advertising or persuasion, and he may even bring in a friend."[5] Deming's example here predates by almost 25 years John Goodman's research about the high value of customers who continue to buy from you.

What happens if a firm does not account for those invisible figures?

In an example that should ring true to most businesspeople, Deming details what can happen when companies rely on visible numbers alone:

The credit department of a company had succeeded in retaining mostly only customers that pay promptly. The credit department had performed well on the job allotted to them. They deserve a good rating. Figures not so visible, it came to light, showed that the credit department had driven to the competition some of their best customers. Top management looked too late at the total cost.[6]

In other words, seduced by its goals and accounting methods, the firm lost several valuable customer relationships. What's wrong with this picture?

We want to be clear. Traditional cost accounting is very valuable to a firm, but when it is the *only* lens through which top management looks, it can create myopia and damage a business.

Technical Skills and Relationship Skills

In the past, many American business people, except for salespeople, were only tangentially focused on relationship building. Instead, many business executives almost solely valued the left-brain skills of analysis, quantification, and process. American business schools created tens of thousands of graduates with those analytical and process skills. *In today's market, though, those skills are necessary but not sufficient.* Currently, the drive for analytical and quantification skills is starting to complement a dramatically growing emphasis on the right-brain activities related to vision, mission, strategy, relationship, and communication. As Daniel Pink, author of *A Whole New Mind*, says:

The keys to the kingdom are changing hands. The future belongs to a very different kind of person with a very different kind of mind—creators and empathizers, pattern recognizers, and meaning makers. These people—artists, inventors, designers, storytellers, caregivers, consolers, big picture thinkers—will now reap society's richest rewards and share its greatest joy.... We are moving from an economy and a society based on the logical, linear, computer-like capabilities of the Information Age to an economy and a society built on the inventive, empathic big-picture capabilities of what's rising in its place, the Conceptual Age.[7]

Part of the reason relationships are becoming more valued in business, especially in Western countries, is that businesses are beginning to understand that creativity and innovation within solid relationships can offer strategic advantages at a time when it is getting more and more difficult for firms to differentiate themselves. In our postindustrial society, it is now easier than ever to create widgets or find employees with deep, specialized skill sets. It is much harder, though, to find people creative and empathetic enough to help your organization work more effectively, to design future offerings, and to connect with your firm's key stakeholders—customers, investors, and employees.

For example, one of the most competent and effective structural engineers we know is a man named Bill Lantz, former owner and president of a company then known as Lantz, Jones, Nebraska (now SMBH, Inc.), a structural engineering company in Columbus, OH. In 2004, Lantz was honored by the College of Engineering at The Ohio State University as a distinguished alumnus. Often referred to as the "engineer's engineer," Lantz is regularly sought out to do the most complicated, difficult projects. Formally trained both as an architect (with a right-brained orientation) and a structural engineer (a richly left-brained job), Lantz recognized early on that analysis and process were not enough; he had to bring right-brain skills, such as vision, design, empathy, and relationship building, if he were to solve complex construction problems. In essence, he had to develop both sides of his brain. Thus, while Lantz is viewed as highly technically competent, clients also value Lantz for his relationship skills.

Lantz today admits those relationship skills were initially under-developed (and his wife agrees), but his dedication to developing his right brain has clearly paid off. Had he not invested in developing those relationship skills, Lantz probably would have been just another solid engineer rather than the distinguished engineer that he is.

When asked to name a project that was particularly successful because of the quality of the relationships, he named the construction of the Knowlton School of the College of Architecture building at The Ohio State University. He believes that the key to the success of that project resulted from the strong relationships within a diverse project team. The team held not only highly productive conversations but also highly productive project meetings, known for their rich dialogue and free exchange of ideas. Everyone was encouraged to voice his or her own needs, and conflicting needs were addressed and coordinated. Conflicts were therefore minimized, and job-site coordination continued the process started in design. The project meetings, in turn, yielded high levels of mutual trust and respect. Whether it was the strength of the relationships that promoted the dialogue or the other way around, we do not know. All we know is that this project was a tremendous success because of the way the project team worked together within the power of their relationships.

Jerry MacArthur Hultin, former United States Under Secretary of the Navy (1997–2000), was president of the Polytechnic Institute of New York University (2005–2012). One of his many responsibilities was to prepare businesspeople—especially technical businesspeople—for their future careers. He tells us about a British friend of his who described some of the challenges of that task by saying:

> Business students go across a spectrum. On one end of the spectrum often are engineers who can sometimes even go all the way to Asperger's syndrome. On the other end of the spectrum are English majors and artists. And what effective managers try to do is act as a bridge between the engineering side and the creative side of this spectrum. The manager's role is helping each side understand what's going on in the other's head.

So part of a good business curriculum is to get engineers to believe that all those words—all this talking, this using of body language to communicate—all these have value. This can be a hard sell because, to many engineers, this kind of communication appears to be nearly worthless—engineers want to know what to do, not how to feel. But some engineers, especially younger engineers, are beginning to see the value of words and vision. It shows up in whether a project gets funded or not. These engineers now see that projects get funded not only because of the intrinsic value of the "thing"—I built the world's best new robot—but also because of the consequences of the thing—the robot's purpose, its value to society, and its total return on investment.[8]

This emphasis on selling your ideas through effective communication—getting the buy-in of both technical and creative sorts—means that engineers, *as well as the rest of us*, must understand and connect with their target audiences. They will almost certainly have to adapt their communication styles and media to succeed, perhaps moving between Twitter notes, technical diagrams, and a formal presentation. They also have to understand fully how sales, operations, finance, research and development (R&D), and executive leadership will use the information provided. This ability to connect with the funding audience, as well as other elements of relationship competence we will be examining, is growing increasingly fundamental to business success in the twenty-first century.

Those highly skilled people who can translate the technical or analytical into a language that elegantly communicates with multiple audiences—technical, nontechnical, executives, and customers—are emerging as the rock stars in the new economy. We know, for example, a business leader who can communicate effectively with both information technology (IT) people and businesspeople; he is always busy because the need for technical translation is always there. Relationships and communication are vital ways to advance your career as well as to increase the number of opportunities available to your businesses. Yet some of us do not actively cultivate or nurture these skills, convincing ourselves that they get in the way of "the work" we desperately need to get done.

For some businesspeople like Bill Lantz (and perhaps for you), the need to invest in developing strong relationship skills is obvious. They see it as a key to their success. These people understand that *people buy from people* and that, as Tom Peters says, "All purchase decisions, all repurchase decisions, hinge, ultimately, on *conversations* and *relationships*."[9] Put more strongly, without solid relationships—both with colleagues and with customers—there would be no sales, no commissions, and no business.

Even fields that are very process driven, such as supply-chain management, rely heavily on relationships. Art van Bodegraven, a colleague in the field of supply-chain management, emphasizes the power of relationships by saying:

> It's all about relationships, in any business, actually, but particularly in supply chain management. Good relationships are pearls without price; bad relationships will definitely limit opportunities for supply chain success. Having relationships that are meaningful, that is, that pay off, demands day-in, day-out hard work. We are saying that the work would be even harder without good relationships.[10]

Many other workers, though, perhaps even you, may be more focused on strong technical background, and the increasing emphasis on developing strong business relationships is a new and often unsettling prospect. For a more technical, more analytical worker, having to grapple with ambiguous and often complex relationship issues can seem messy or frivolous. Technical folks tend to favor the powerful language of finance or the elegance of a Venn diagram, an elaborate flowchart, or a process map. These things are tangible—unlike concepts such as *rapport* and *trust* and even *effective relationships*.

Businesspeople who work at becoming more authentic and more skillful relationship builders are in many cases those who get promoted and succeed in reaching their goals. We know of an electrical engineer who was a gifted leader and developer of relationships. His career skyrocketed because he was a very rare bird in a primarily engineering environment. His managers in many cases could not say exactly what he was doing to succeed, but they couldn't argue with his results.

When Business Cultures Value Technical and People Skills: Bottom-Line Results

What happens in business cultures that recognize how important technical and people skills are? To answer that question, John P. Kotter and James Heskett studied dozens of corporate cultures and concluded, in *Corporate Culture and Performance*, that

> Corporate culture can have a significant impact on a firm's long-term economic performance. We found that firms with cultures that emphasized all the key managerial constituencies (customers, stockholders and employees) and leadership from managers at all levels outperformed firms that did not have those cultural traits by a huge margin. Over an eleven-year period, the former increased revenues by an average of 682 percent versus 166 percent for the latter, expanded their work forces by 282 percent versus 36 percent, grew their stock prices by 901 percent versus 74 percent, and improved their net incomes by 756 percent versus 1 percent.[11]

When Kotter and Heskett speak of constituencies, they are speaking about critical relationships. We agree with them that the relationship advantage can offer a major competitive differentiation. When people or businesses have this advantage, they can thrive. We'll examine Southwest Airlines a bit later, as well as Medtronics and other firms that have used a relationship strategy to differentiate themselves.

Increases, over an 11-year period

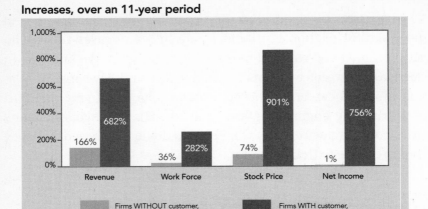

Corporate Culture and Performance, Kotter 2011

So Does This Mean You Need to Learn to Schmooze?

Probably not, but it depends on what you mean by *schmoozing*. Originally, schmoozing meant sharing a rumor or gossiping. For some these days, schmoozing is about "gripping and grinning," manipulating, and impressing. This meaning implies that you might be inauthentic to get what you want. Clearly, if this is what you think of what is meant by schmoozing, avoid it at all costs. It certainly won't help you to create empowering relationships, and it may cause you to lose many of those you already have. Few people want to be seen as a manipulator or fraud. That type of approach ultimately catches up with you.

On the other hand, if you think of schmoozing as authentically making others feel special, welcome, or of value, then have at it! If you've ever been new to a group or a job, you know how helpful it can be to have someone introduce you around and show you the ropes. In our experience, though, people described as schmoozers are often just extroverts on steroids. They have a great many close friends and love to be around people. For them, getting to know someone new is exciting. It's energizing. They genuinely want to learn about others and make them feel welcome. They are great at networking and hosting a gathering. We have a colleague whose idea of a great party is going into a room with 100+ people she has never met. To her, that is a blast. Some of the rest of us, facing such a situation, would rather have unanesthetized dental work. So if you're an extrovert, connecting with others comes naturally. For those who are introverts, learning how to connect with others in a more systematic way may be the key to their success. Let's look at two types of relationship builders who each create powerful relationships. Consider two different types of relationship power by looking at two different types of realtors, Mary and Don.

Mary's focus was on "doing the deal." She was a good but very transactional realtor. She could be quite successful but was more capable of hitting singles than home runs. If our friend Tom was looking to purchase or lease a single office, he would go to Mary immediately because the source of her relationship power was the large number of names in her contact database. She knew everyone in town. Talking with her would be the quickest way to find out who had a single office and might want financing.

If, however, Tom was looking to purchase or lease a large building, he would almost certainly go to Don. Don, the top commercial real estate producer in the city, also had a good contact database, but he had mostly deep, long-term relationships that ensured his continued success. Unlike Mary, who enjoyed being the center of attention, Don had a quiet presence that people noticed the minute he entered a room. Some would say that he had "personal power." He listened more than he spoke, and people trusted him on a number of levels. He was particularly good at ferreting out all of a prospect's specific realty needs. He was so good at listening and so committed to his prospect's needs that he would not show buildings *first*, as most realtors do. Rather, he would write a description of what he understood as the prospect's needs and challenges, and then he would confirm or revise it with the client. Then—and only then—would he offer to show buildings. Thus neither party wasted time, and both had a common vision and mission as they began working together, thus making the project much more likely to succeed.

So which of these roles would you rather play? Both Mary and Don build powerful business relationships, but the source of their power and the nature of their relationships are considerably different. Mary gets her power by making *a great many* connections, knowing "the right people," and perhaps sometimes telling people what they want to hear. She is always "in the know." Don, on the other hand, gets his power focusing on fewer, longer-term relationships. People like Don are often more interested in their prospects and customers than they are in themselves. They will sometimes, for example, send a prospect to a specialist, splitting their commission, so that the customer gets exactly what he needs. People trust and respect relationship builders like Don. So how would you like to be known? Either approach to relationship power can bring you success, but the practices you need to develop will differ.

How Do We Assess the Power of Business Relationships?

When we assess the power of a company's business relationships, we examine the interplay among four elements:

1. The *interactions between individuals within groups*—teams, divisions, suppliers, and customers
2. The *organizational structures and infrastructures*—reporting relationships, project structures, goals, measures, compensation, and processes that support or inhibit those interpersonal interactions
3. The *culture*—especially the values and cultural norms
4. The alignment of all the above to support the firm's strategy

We have learned during almost three decades of helping to build or repair business relationships that we need to take a broader perspective when we are trying to improve business results. This is so because *relationships don't exist in isolation.* Rather, they are part of a system that can either support or negate any progress made. To better understand what we mean, let's look briefly at each of the four elements we assess.

Individual and Team Interactions

Effective interactions between individuals depend on how people treat each other individually *within the contexts* of teams, divisions, departments, suppliers, and customers. Our experience has been that dysfunctional personal relationships can damage all these group relationships no matter how hard people work to solve the individual and firm challenges. Without healthy relationships, especially within teams, problem solvers can become like the mythical Sisyphus, endlessly rolling a huge stone up a hill, watching it roll back down, and then having to roll it up all over again. Most businesspeople have felt like this at some point in their careers.

But fixing individual or team relationships often will not solve the problem. There is often more than one force at play. This is why we also look at organizational structure and culture.

Organizational Structures

Organizational structures and *infrastructures* either support or inhibit individual and group interactions. Often companies have such strong functional reporting relationships and project teams that they soon find themselves working in silos, with few, if any, cross-functional or boundary-spanning processes or relationships. What we often see is that R&D designs a new product. They "throw it over the wall" to manufacturing, which, in turn, throws it over the wall to marketing, and then marketing throws it over the wall to sales. You probably know how it feels to get things dumped on you. In these types of companies, soon there can be a great many customer complaints because the right hand doesn't know (or sometimes doesn't care) what the left hand is doing. This leads to rework, waste, and frustration. Some would call this a process problem. We would also call it a relationship problem that may have been caused in part by a lack of cross-functional communication and/or in part was created by the rigid organizational structure.

At one manufacturing company we knew, manufacturing got involved in a battle with sales because the two compensation systems worked against each other. This resulted in wasting enormous time and energy and damaged business results. Both the organizational structure and the infrastructures, especially the competing compensation systems, significantly contributed to the relationship and performance issues.

Culture

We have talked about how personal interactions and organizational structure affect relationships and performance. Now let's turn to the impact of culture. Culture is formed by the beliefs, values, traditions, or norms (both written and unwritten) that define the context in which relationships exist and drive behavior. Some are so powerful that if they are followed, people get promoted, but if they are broken, they can get people fired.

How do the cultural norms in your business work? Does your business's culture value showing respect to other people, or does it tolerate people being publically berated? Does it value and promote self-awareness through training and coaching, or does it see that as a waste of money? Does your culture have structures and initiatives that promote cross-functional collaboration or have structures that reinforce silos and end up pitting individuals and departments against each other?

Dr. James B. Thomas, Elliott Professor of Risk and Management at the Smeal College of Business at The Pennsylvania State University, comments on the power of culture:

> [When getting to know people], we are always [incorrectly] assuming some sort of contextual independence. What do I mean by that? We know that people coming out of organization X are going to think a certain way and differently from those from organization Y. The culture—the context that particular organization

drives—will grind a lens through which they see the world and business relationships. If you are coming from an organization that is very aggressive, the nature of that relationship will be aggressive. Much like if you are coming from an organization that is defending its markets, you will probably get up on the battlements.... If you assume the people are acting independently (of their corporate cultures) and if you just think of this as a generic business relationship, then you have not done your homework and considered what kind of context is really driving how they view the world. That's a bad mistake. It's a really bad mistake![12]

When seeking to understand cultural norms, we learn the most not by just listening to what people say, but more important, by *watching what they do*. Perhaps the BP oil spill in the Gulf of Mexico can teach us something about the importance of cultural values. In April 2010, the Deepwater Horizon rig exploded, "killing 11, injuring 17, and spewing at least 3 million barrels of oil into the Gulf of Mexico in what would end up being the greatest environmental disaster in American history."[13] The Baker Report[14] had started tracking BP's cuts in the areas of safety and disaster control in 2007. The results of those cuts, according to Murray Bryant and Trevor Hunter, writing in the *Ivey Business Journal*, suggested that the Deepwater tragedy might have been prevented had the BP culture been more responsible, saying:

> BP's horrible missteps after the Deepwater Horizon rig exploded were almost predictable, given the culture of deceit and arrogance that executive actions had encouraged. While the accident could have been prevented, BP might have avoided its intense and deserved public flogging if only it had respected the best practices for managing a crisis—and for managing.[15]

How much has it cost BP for its decision to cut costs and corners? The company has already paid tens of billions of dollars, and the reckoning is nowhere near complete.

Organizational Alignment

Finally, *alignment* means that everything—people, structure, culture—works together to support the firm's strategy. Peter Rouse, author of *Every Relationship Matters*, says that alignment:

> [i]s the means by which the individual and the collective (the people in your firm) generate, release, and share energy. By energy I am referring to such qualities as willingness, enthusiasm, creativity, and innovation. The importance of these energetic qualities is easily understood by simply imagining where you or your business would be without any one of them. The complete absence of energy is rare; more commonly it is simply in short supply.[16]

Misalignment means that your firm is fighting against itself. Sadly, it happens more frequently than most like to admit; our guess is that somewhere in your professional life you have experienced misalignment and seen the resulting inefficiencies and loss of productivity.

In review, assessing the health and power of business relationships causes us to examine (1) personal interactions within and among teams, (2) organizational structure and infrastructure, (3) culture, and (4) the alignment of all these relationships around the firm's strategy. When all these are working in concert, the company is powerfully positioned for strong results and a competitive advantage. The business has unleashed its power through the power of its business relationships.

Benefits for Your Organization: Relationships and Alignment

Dr. James B. Thomas the Elliott Professor of Risk and Management at the Smeal College of Business at The Pennsylvania State University, and prior to this he served as dean of the Pennsylvania State College of Information Sciences and Technology (1999–2006) and dean of the Pennsylvania State Smeal College of Business (2006–2012). His broad wealth of experience leads him to say:

> There are, I think, two critical keys to organizational success that oftentimes are overlooked. One of those keys is understanding relationships—within and outside of the firm. It's about recognizing the role that the human spirit plays in defining and implementing relationships from operational to external business links. It's not just numbers; oftentimes it's not numbers at all. It is about recognizing the emotional expectations that people have in interactions as opposed to (or perhaps better: in addition to) their business or technical expectations. In many ways, it is that recognition that significantly contributes to defining the notion of *exceptional* leadership at any level.
>
> The second key is aligning the organization. This goes well beyond, for example, the basic needs of coordinating processes and technology. It is about linking strategy (e.g., vision, mission, goals) to culture (e.g., core values, identity, community) through ongoing actions and setting of examples; and using that drive for fit and linkage as criteria in decision making. Starbucks, Google, Nordstrom's, and Disney are examples of how this gets operationalized and how it can contribute to success. In the end, great leaders push their organizations (however defined) by defending and advocating for these two elements of success.[17]

Being able to create and align these authentic and powerful business relationships gets you validation and appreciation. Thus your technical skills, whatever they are, *and* your relationship skills, can get you the recognition you deserve.

As we've said before, empowering business relationships enable you and your company to grow and thrive. Look for a second at customer relationships. In the seventies and eighties, John Goodman, who founded the Technical Assistance Research Program (TARP), quantified the fact that

[i]t costs five times as much to get a new customer as it does to keep one. The original analysis ... was based on looking at how much General Motors was spending to advertise to get a new customer versus how much they would have spent to solve a problem to retain a customer. That's where the 5-to-1 ratio came from and that was very conservative because it didn't include a whole range of other marketing expenses.... For business-to-business, it's not five times as much; it's probably 20 to 50 times as much.[18]

Creating and maintaining powerful, authentic relationships equates with incremental dollars.

Putting It All Together: Southwest Airlines— Relationship Competence at Work

Let's examine one business in which relationships are valued and optimized: Southwest Airlines. Southwest, which has had tremendous success in a hypercompetitive industry, has based its firm culture on what it calls "relational competence."[19]

This means that relationships with the union, with shareholders, with partners, and with individual employees are conducted with respect, trust, and openness. If we look at Southwest's hiring practices alone, one of the critical job criteria is having this relational competence. When relational competence is defined, it comes down to certain behaviors, among which are the ability to

 Empathize (show respect for others)

 Listen carefully (and not interrupt)

 Demonstrate a disposition to help others

Other firms might scoff at such criteria, but for decades it has worked for Southwest.

Let's focus on bottom-line results. Since the airline was founded in 1967, it has consistently been the most profitable carrier in its industry. Not coincidentally, Southwest also has its industry's fastest turnaround times. As Jody Hoffer Gittell says:

> Southwest is the only airline to have won the airline industry's "Triple Crown"—the fewest delays, the fewest complaints, and the fewest mishandled bags—not only for individual months but for entire years, from 1992 to 1996. . . . No other airline has won . . . more than one month at a time.[20]

One of the major reasons the firm has been so successful in turnarounds is the coordination of its teams.

Simply examine the Southwest turnaround team. While Southwest's competitors usually have 11 people responsible for

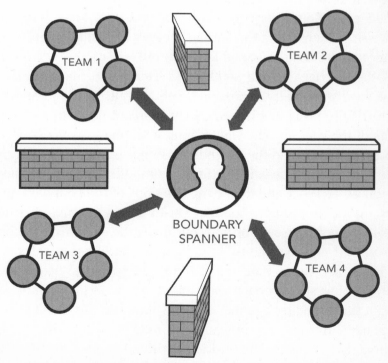

Southwest's boundary spanner facilitating communication within organization.

departures, Southwest's team has an extra person—a twelfth— called a *boundary spanner*,[21] whose job is to coordinate the tasks of the entire team. This boundary spanner is ultimately responsible for on-time takeoffs. As Jody Hoffer Gittell says:

> relational coordination resulted in fewer delays, fewer lost bags, faster turnarounds, and higher employee productivity in a study comparing operations at Southwest, United, Continental, and American. Although relationships are relatively "soft" organizational factors and therefore tempting to neglect under challenging conditions, relationships of shared goals, shared knowledge and mutual respect contribute *substantially* to effective coordination and therefore to quality and efficiency performance.[22]

Although business travelers originally were not Southwest's target market, we and our business friends have increasingly experienced Southwest's superior performance. More and more professionals are using this airline because of customer treatment, faster turnaround times, and fewer overall hassles.

Other carriers, noting Southwest's excellent turnaround times, have tried to copy its approach. Some of Southwest's competitors even tried to bring in a boundary spanner, but no matter what the skills of the spanner, she was dealing with team members who in most cases respected their own competence much more than their team's responsibilities. At Southwest, all the employees—including the pilots—respect and follow the decisions of the boundary spanners. At other airlines, boundary-spanner impersonators simply lacked the power to develop and coordinate the relationships among the other 11 people responsible for boarding and on-time takeoff.

The other thing that crippled the competitors' attempts to copy Southwest's approach was that other carriers could not cost-justify the boundary spanner as a full-time job. They loaded extra responsibilities on spanners, undermining their effectiveness and ultimately wiping out the position entirely. For now, it's enough to say that Southwest's focus on relational skills has unleashed the

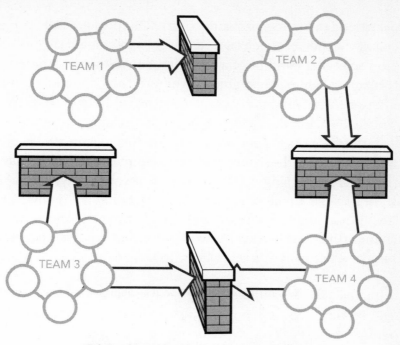

Relationships without boundary spanner in place.

power that has created a rare healthy bottom line in a tail-spinning industry. We believe that relational competence is a competitive differentiator—and a powerful one—for Southwest Airlines. This may be so in part because few other organizations see relational competence as a skill worth fighting for.

How Do Relationships Work? The Social Exchange Theory

You can learn a lot about how relationships work by considering the implications of social exchange theory. Vernon L. Smith, a Nobel Prize winner in economics (2002) for his ground-breaking research in behavioral economics, influenced a whole new field of research in exchange theory. Although Smith's research was done primarily in the 1950s, in the 1960s a number of people in economics, psychology, and communication started asking if there were social implications to Smith's exchange theory. They asked: Did such an exchange happen between two people or two companies?

The emerging concept of a social exchange theory is based on a number of factors, chief among which is the notion of *reciprocity*. Put one way, reciprocity means that when I help you, there is an implied assumption that—if you want a relationship—you will return the favor. As the theory developed, this reciprocity became, "I will help you to the extent that you help me." You can hear this sort of exchange going on when a businessperson says, "I had to cash in a whole bunch of chits to solve that one" or "He owed me a few." What people are referring to here is the concept of social exchange. The trick, however, is to understand what the other party values, by what social currency he is driven.

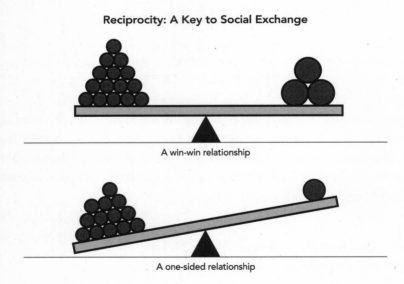

Reciprocity: A Key to Social Exchange

A win-win relationship

A one-sided relationship

To understand what *social currencies* means, we need to look at the various currencies valued by individuals. Allan R. Cohen and David L. Bradford explain the theory and the notion of social currencies in their book, *Influence Without Authority*. What they call social currencies helps each of us to better understand our own social currency, what we value when building a relationship.

Although the authors identify five social currencies, what is important is that people trade in different currencies. In other words, *not everyone wants or values the same thing in a relationship*. For example, some are motivated by inspiration-related currencies. These people value such things as making a difference, doing something well, or doing the right thing. Others value such things as having access to new resources, learning new skills or solving new problems, getting faster responses, and so on. In other words, these people value task-related currencies. Still others value prestige or recognition or understanding and acceptance or such things as gratitude or freedom from hassles. So you can quickly see how different people value different currencies in a social exchange.[23]

You can see this most clearly when you look at the struggle to build effective employee recognition programs. Being singled out and called to the front of an auditorium to receive an award is highly motivating for some but terrifying for others who trade in a different currency. Providing implementation assistance to one person who values resources and support can be seen as a gift; to another, who values being recognized as competent, that offer may be seen as an insult. Trying to understand what motivates another person and learning what she values in a relationship is no small thing. It helps if you can ask the person questions designed to uncover her preferred currency rather than simply relying on your own guess about what might be important to her.

Increasing your personal power by influencing without authority requires effort and practice. You have to be self-aware enough to know what currencies you trade in, as well as being able to determine the social currencies of others. This requires getting to know your fellow workers better—a good thing in and of itself—so that you can target your offers to their currencies. Once you can do that, you can become what Rosabeth Moss Kanter sees as a "business hero" who can "learn to operate without the might of authority behind [you]. The crutch of authority must be thrown away and replaced by [your] own personal ability to make relationships, use influence, and work with others to achieve results."[24]

How Is the Landscape of Relationships Changing?

One of the elements that is rapidly changing in business relationships is the number of channels through which we can work with others to achieve results. Historically, business relationships were formed eye to eye, with a meeting and a handshake. Today, in an increasingly digital world, businesses and their employees have the opportunity to connect with more diverse kinds of information, potential partners, clients, and collaborators than ever before. These connections often occur through existing online communication platforms and communities, then can evolve into face-to-face meetings. Online information has become so ubiquitous that many of us have a hard time remembering on which platform certain relationships started. Did I follow that person on Twitter before I met him at last month's Meetup (an online group meeting-facilitator network)? Was I introduced through one of my connections on LinkedIn, or did he respond to one of my Facebook posts? Did he attend one of my previous webinars, or did we meet at last quarter's industry conference?

With the increase in the number of relationships we are developing because of technology, prioritization of those relationships is becoming a valuable skill. Derek Smith, former chairman and CEO of ChoicePoint, a data aggregation company that acted as a private intelligence service to government and industry, gave us his approach to segmenting them, saying,

> You have to learn to prioritize relationships. You have only so much time and effort both in time and emotionally that you can give to various relationships. So all relationships aren't the same. You need to learn early on as to which relationships are ones that are permanent, which ones are situational, and which ones are very transitory and which ones quite frankly don't need to be developed at all. It's a very complex skill to be able to prioritize time when either everybody wants your attention or people can't get your attention long enough to help you adequately determine with

whom, why and when to build a meaningful relationship. This process takes experience and an extraordinary amount of effort.[25]

Similarly, relationship dynamics within organizations are shifting with the adoption of internal communication tools such as SalesForce's Chatter and Microsoft's Yammer. Although the original goal of social networks was to enable faster information exchange and communication between employees, it is interesting to note how such networks affect the relationships that are formed as a result. Text-based technologies undoubtedly have their limitations and can fall short when conveying nuances such as sarcasm, happiness, surprise, or urgency—causing the mood of a conversation and ultimately the strength of a relationship between individuals to shift over time.

How different generations see and use the new technologies also can prevent relationships from forming to their full potential. An older CEO may view employees using Facebook at work as a waste of company time, even though the junior-level account managers are setting up private groups to facilitate file sharing and live chatting with team members to get faster and clearer responses than those from e-mail.

It is, however, important to be aware that technology (i.e., e-mail, pagers, cell phones, social networks, and videoconferences) will change over time (probably by tomorrow) and will continue to affect the way we communicate and connect with our friends, family, coworkers, and business contacts. Failing to monitor and examine how people use these tools to facilitate relationships would be as naive as not recognizing that we use different personal communication styles.

The platform for relationship building will require different strategies, but we believe that the emphasis on business relationships is going to remain central to the success of most businesses. As Benjamin Franklin once said, in a different context, "We either hang together or we most assuredly will hang separately."[26]

POINTS TO REMEMBER

Overview

>> Relationships do not exist in isolation. Rather, there are four main elements that affect relationships:
- Individual and team interactions
- Organizational structures and infrastructures
- Cultural norms
- Alignment

>> Powerful business relationships can significantly affect your personal effectiveness, as well as your impact on your team and organization.

>> Although long undervalued, companies today are placing a greater amount of emphasis on "soft skills" as they once did on "hard skills." Consider how this affects the way you are positioned within your team or organization.

>> Social exchange theory, in particular the concept of reciprocity, affects the dynamics of both personal and business relationships.

>> Empowering relationships drive company productivity, profitability, and competetive advantage.

For Individuals

>> It is a combination of your technical skills and your relationship skills that will help to get you the recognition you deserve.

>> Which would you rather be, a transactional or long-term relationship builder? Does your personality lend itself to one over the other? If so, what could you learn or incorporate from the other?

>> Which side of your brain is more prominent? What can you do to strengthen the other side to create a more balanced approach so you can build relationships with a wider range of people?

For Teams

» How does your preferred communication style affect your relationship with team members?

» Southwest has the best turnaround time in the airline industry thanks in part to the way it structures its teams. In your industry, what is the analog for turnaround time? What are the three major ways that your industry's most important customers judge their suppliers? How are you doing in those three areas, and how might you improve your performance in any of them?

 For Organizations

» Do a simple math exercise to determine how valuable some of your relationships are. Take your three largest customer relationships. How much is each of those accounts worth over the next 5 to 10 years? Compare those revenue totals with how much you are currently investing in developing and growing those relationships. If there is a large disparity between those numbers (and there almost always is), then ask those who manage those account relationships what investments need to be made to grow that account. Using their lifetime value to your firm, justify some of those investments.

» How is the alignment (or lack thereof) affecting the relationships in and around your organization?

NOTES

_____

_____

_____

_____

_____

_____

Connect First; Then Focus on Task

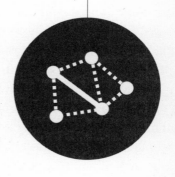

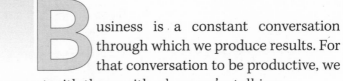

usiness is a constant conversation through which we produce results. For that conversation to be productive, we need to first connect with those with whom we're talking.

Why Connect?

The world of business is fast-paced and intense. We have to get too much done in too little time. Thus we become focused on getting the work done quickly and efficiently. In this context the idea of business people stopping to connect first and then focusing on task may seem counterproductive. Thus in our hurly-burly business lives, it's easy to forget that our work usually gets done with and through others—no matter how technical our work may be. If we focus purely on task, we risk producing second-class work.

You may have heard someone say, "Get back to work," when she saw people standing in the kitchen area or by a water cooler talking, no matter the nature of the conversation. That person believes that talking is not "working" and therefore a waste of time. In doing this, she fails to understand that business is a constant conversation through which we share ideas and get work done. And those conversations are meant to connect people. As Daniel Goleman says:

> The most fundamental revelation of the new discipline [brain science]: we are wired to connect. Neuroscience has discovered that our brain's very design makes it *sociable*, inexorably drawn into an intimate brain-to-brain linkup whenever we engage with another person. That neural bridge lets us affect the brain—and so the body—of everyone we interact with, just as they do us.[1]

We have to connect to work together most effectively. When we meet a businessperson whom we do not know but with whom we may work, we should begin looking for ways to connect—things we might have in common so that we can relate to each other. For example, we often initiate conversations with new people by asking questions about their background and interests: Where did you grow up? What do you do? How long have you lived in this city? What do you like to do for fun? How did you decide to get into this kind of work? And sometimes we start by learning about what they do in their jobs or what their role is on the project or team.

Unlike those who want to quickly move to task, skillful relationship builders can spend a great deal of time learning about the person and finding common interests. They know that investing their time in this way will bring benefit in several ways:

>> They will be better able to decide to what extent they want *or need* to invest in building a deeper relationship with this person.

>> They better understand how this person thinks and what he or she values so that they will be better able to work or communicate with this person.

>> They know that because they have established common ground, they will be better able to solve problems more quickly.

Finding common interests or experiences may help us to later resolve issues, pursue common goals, or open new doors. As Jim Hallett, CEO of KAR Auction Services, said:

For me, it's always relationship before task [our italics]. When I get on an airplane . . . I acknowledge that flight attendant and I speak to her. I develop a relationship the minute I walk on the airplane.[2]

Yet establishing relationships is not simply a matter of courtesy. When asked what connecting with another person allows Jim to do, he replied:

First, I have a very difficult time doing business with people that I don't feel I have a comfortable relationship with. And then a relationship gives you permission to ask for the business. . . . It earns you a better opportunity.[3]

Jim is not talking about manipulation—that's not what he is interested in. Instead, he is genuinely curious about others. He wants to get to know them on a deeper level, quickly learning their story: who they are, where they come from, what they need and want. In describing himself, Jim said:

I want to know how you arrived. I say it is amazing. Everybody comes from somewhere. And we all have a very unique story, . . . and I want to know it. Steve or Jake has a unique story, and I want to know that. And when I can know that story, not only have I shown interest in you, I've learned about you. And you appreciated the opportunity I've given you . . . to talk about yourself, which we all like to do.[4]

We asked Jim what would happen if one of his potential business partners just wanted to move straight to task. He told us the following story:

I traveled to another part of the world and met with a father and a son. We were going to talk with them because we wanted to discuss the possibility of buying their business. The father, Max, was 75 years old, and his son, Amos, was in his 40s. Max immediately came across as a crusty old guy. We hadn't sat down for five minutes when he asked, "So Jim, how much are you going to pay me for my business? Let's cut right to the chase."

And I said, "That's interesting, Max. I thought we'd take a *little* longer to get to that. Truthfully, Max, I don't normally go there in the first five minutes, but typically what we pay is based on X, Y and Z. . . . So with that said, why don't we just back up and first get to know each other a little bit better, talk about your business, you and your son."[5]

Jim told us that he had to make a judgment call:

Do I insist on connecting first, or does Max need some information first before he feels comfortable sharing information with me about himself? So I made the call and gave Max enough information to satisfy him. Then we were able to go back and get to know each other better. And knowing more about Max and his son will make a huge difference in our decision as to whether or not we decide to invest in his business.[6]

That is about meeting someone new. When meeting a business-person they haven't seen in a while, though, skillful relationship builders like Jim Hallett, Jerry Hultin, and Bill Lantz, do something a little different. They always take time to reconnect. The questions they might ask in this situation are similar to but not the same as they ask folks they don't know. When reconnecting, they might ask:

>> What's happened since I last saw you?
>> How is your family?
>> How in the world did you solve that problem we worked on last week so quickly?
>> What are you working on these days?

Some people call this *small talk*, but in many ways there is nothing small about it, especially in business. It's the lifeblood of business.

This reconnecting *reinforces our relationship*; it helps us catch up with one another *before* we turn to the task at hand. It demonstrates that *we care about one another as human beings*. It both acknowledges our unique lives and yet reestablishes a shared understanding and/or experience. When we meaningfully connect with others, we feel validated and valued. We find a piece of ground from which we can mutually navigate and negotiate. We feel safer. Why? Because we feel free to be ourselves, to say what we honestly think, and to take risks. In short, we become energized.

In social settings, we usually first take time to reconnect. In business, however, driven by our need to be efficient, our temptation is too often to simply cut out the small talk and move straight to task: "It's time to get the meeting started. Let's get going. How are we doing with implementing the new tracking system?" This is our attempt to get from point A to point B in the shortest distance. In doing so, we may fail to realize the barriers that may impede or slow our progress.

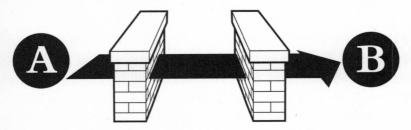

Hidden relationship barriers that exist between tasks.

In this situation, we too often forget that most "work" gets done through relationships. Thus, paradoxically, the failure to connect with our colleagues, suppliers, and clients actually can slow us down and cost us—and others—*big time*! Without opening the lines of communication and identifying obstacles first, we sometimes force ourselves to struggle through issues that could have been easily avoided.

Better relationships reduce barriers and enable more efficient ways to work.

A Business Leader Learns the Importance of Connecting

A Fortune 100 financial services company executive, whom we'll call Maureen, recently asked us to attend a meeting that she was holding to address a stalled mission-critical technology project. She wanted some feedback about how she could resolve an impasse with her team.

Maureen had grown increasingly frustrated with Jeff, the technology lead, who seemed disengaged and unaware of the urgent need to get things back on track. Although she and other team members had talked with him one-on-one, nothing seemed to help. Things were moving toward a crisis. The project was at risk of running over budget and missing the first of a series of deadlines. This meeting needed to turn things around. Let's watch what happened:

When the meeting began, the tension in the room was obvious to all. Before beginning the meeting, though, Maureen took a deep breath and paused a moment. She smiled, sat back, panned around the table looking everyone directly in the eye, and said: "It's good to see you. I'm glad you're here. I desperately need each and every one of you to make this project a success. I know we have a packed agenda, but before we jump in, I'd like to take a minute and just check in. How are you doing? *Is there anything that might be getting in the way of your being fully present in this meeting that we should know about?"*

A few people made light-hearted comments. Then Jeff, the technology lead, spoke: "Sorry guys. I want to be here, but I've been having a hard time concentrating these days. I know I've been disengaged, but my four-year-old daughter has not been doing well for a couple of months. I kept having this nagging feeling that something was terribly wrong, and then yesterday we had to take her to the hospital for some pretty serious tests. The doctors think she'll be okay, but they are supposed to call me this afternoon to give me the test results. So I'm going to leave my phone on, and if I get that call, I'm going to step out. I am committed to this project hitting a home run, so I promise to catch up or else get someone top-notch to pinch hit for me. Just for a little bit today, though, I need you to understand where my head's at."

The relief in the room was palpable. Everyone finally understood that Jeff had been committed but preoccupied. They knew that he would pull through and do whatever it took to make the project a success. They let him know that they supported him and then got to work. It was one of their most productive meetings because once connected, they were focused solidly on the task. They had more information, so they could create backup plans if needed and identify things they could do to fast-track the project. In the end, Maureen's remembering to connect first saved the meeting—and the project. She had practiced a key move: *Connect first; then move to task*. We just got to see what a difference her move made.

Later, when we met with her to debrief the meeting, she told us that in that moment at the beginning of the meeting when she paused, she suddenly remembered other meetings during which extraneous issues had derailed the meeting even before it began— times when people were confused about the meeting's purpose, when someone had an outdated document with them, or when someone was physically but not mentally present.

She told us that she knew that even though time was of the essence, thanks to our earlier conversations, she realized that *she had to make a new move* at the beginning of this meeting to make certain that everyone was on the same page. This meeting had to work; she had to break through the blockage impeding this project. She had suddenly remembered the importance of *connecting first* and wondered if, by taking a minute to give everyone an opportunity to check in first, whatever had been holding Jeff or the others back might rise to the surface. Thankfully, the story had a happy ending on several levels, but it might have gone very differently. Many of us have seen buried issues sinking a critical meeting. Can you imagine

>> How things might have gone if Maureen had not stopped and taken the time to connect first?

>> What the tone of the meeting might have become?
>> How the team would have reacted if Jeff had suddenly left the room to take a call?
>> How differently things might have turned out for everyone?

Taking time to connect first, acknowledging team members, and then turning to task can make a world of difference in certain types of situations. Look how much time Maureen and the team wasted by not really understanding the load Jeff was carrying—two months! Had they discovered and addressed this issue with Jeff earlier, they could have planned and executed their project differently and more quickly.

Physical Connection and Mental Presence

As we saw in the preceding example, failing to connect first enabled Jeff to be *physically but not mentally* present. Keep in mind that people don't need a major event to become preoccupied. For example, if you've just remembered something important that you have forgotten to do, or you've received an unsettling e-mail from a family member, or you're worrying about some recurring personal or professional issue, it is tough to be *mentally* present. Hard as we may try, sometimes it takes a minute or more to actually switch our mental gears and focus on the task at hand.

Skilled businesspeople understand this, so they take a minute at the beginning of a conversation or meeting to connect. They build in time to check in briefly before they move on with the conversation or meeting agenda. This check-in, or reconnection time, allows people to let others know that they're present but may be struggling to stay focused. Clearly, there has to be enough trust in the room for people to feel safe sharing what's going on in their lives, but given that, sharing in the meeting makes it possible for everyone to be mentally and physically present when the meeting starts. People don't have to share details of the issue, but it is freeing to be able to let others know that we're preoccupied. It both helps us let go of what we've been struggling with and also reduces the likelihood that others will misinterpret our behavior. Because we have taken the time to connect, everyone can focus—to the best of their ability—on the task at hand and move forward.

Connecting First Saves Time and Gets Better Results in the Long Run

Let's be clear: when we suggest that one key to building a powerful business relationship is to connect first and *then* focus on task, we *are not* suggesting that *all* business conversations begin with comments about the weather, last night's game, or compliments on someone's success. Those things are mostly ice breakers or warm-ups. Instead, we are suggesting that if you take the time to check in or connect with someone on a personal level before you start to work with that person, it *may get you better results.* This may be especially true when

>> You are working with people you don't know well or haven't seen for a long time
>> The topic at hand is likely to be sensitive or contentious
>> Something seems off—not quite right, or
>> You need to solve a problem quickly

An honest "How are you doing today?" and *really* wanting to know the answer, a "What's happening?" and a "What's new with you?" are the kinds of questions we can ask to connect with people we don't know well or haven't seen for a while. Connecting first may yield big payoffs in saving time and working together more effectively. Through these authentic questions, *we can actually learn something* about the other person that could enable us to adapt our approach or our agenda or simply acknowledge that we appreciate the person's situation. Often just being able to say what is true for us at a given moment is enough to let us move on. For us, an inescapable conclusion in the twenty-first century is that *the greatest gift we can bestow on another person is our undivided attention.* People have a deep need to be acknowledged, and they become more energized and engaged on those too-rare occasions when it happens. Connecting first can engage that energy.

Connecting First Starts to Build Trust

Dr. Peter Goldsmith, associate professor and Interim Director of the Food and Agribusiness Management Program at the University of Illinois, and an internationally recognized expert in food-science agribusiness, faced a particularly daunting challenge in a very rural town in an emerging country. He had been asked to introduce artificial insemination into cattle, but few of the farmers knew much about this new science. As Goldsmith recalls:

> I was working in the area of animal husbandry and artificial insemination. *I knew I had to start by trying to understand where people were coming from.* In this case, if a farmer has a sick cow or a sick horse, he's got real issues. For these people, cows are their livelihood!
>
> First, I began by building relationships with the farmers, by talking with them about the technology, which was mostly unknown there. Only a couple of people had ever heard of it, so I found leaders of the community who could more easily explain the technology behind artificial insemination. They had credibility with their fellow farmers.
>
> Once you prove you can speak their language—both figuratively and literally—others then start to listen to you. They see that you are working in their city or town. You are living there. They see that you're giving your all. You are not a phony, and that starts to build trust. It's at this point that they start to make an investment in you and the technology. Because they were putting their cows together to create one large herd, they were taking a lot of risk with me.[7]

How Can I Learn to Connect First?

Unless they have some psychological disorder, most people learn to connect from their parents, friends, or colleagues. Others mold themselves by watching master business relationship builders. Paula Marshall, Chair and CEO, The Bama Companies, Inc., learned this lesson from her parents. She told us:

INDIVIDUAL

I learned at the feet of my father and my mother. My dad used to tell me, "You're the only one that wants to hear about you. Everyone else wants to talk about themselves. So when you go out to sell, the first thing you must do is find out about the other person. You want to engage them. You want to get them talking."

One of the best ways I found to build new relationships is to ask them about their family. We might be sitting in an office trying to put together a deal for a new production plant in China or Europe somewhere. Some people call it small talk, but I usually find it the most interesting conversation of the whole meeting. You're learning about that person, who they are, what makes them who they are today. And you are dealing with that person today.

If you're dealing with someone who is having a rough day because they've got a child or a parent or a relationship they are worried about, you might not get the best of them that day. When you engage them in the beginning about themselves, they might even tell you, "Well, I'm kind of having a bad day today. I've got some issues that I'm dealing with, and I apologize if I need to go out to make a phone call or if I'm a little distant or something." It makes you more real to them and them more real to you.

You can't just say, "Hi, my name is Paula Marshall—tell me about your family." *You have to work up to it.* "Well how long have you been in this job? What part of the job do you really like?"

We just got a new buyer in one of our relationships with a large customer. She is from Russia, so we've spent some very quality time just talking to her and getting to know her. And it was fascinating listening to her talk about growing up in Russia and how she got out of there. She got out because she was smart. She educated herself and got a finance degree. Then she applied for different programs, and she left Russia, and now she's over here in the States and has a couple of MBAs and is getting another Masters. You just sit there and go, "Wow, I would have never known that if we hadn't engaged at that level."[8]

There are those who learn relationship building by watching relationship experts and/or by asking them what they did to develop their ability to connect with others. Frequently, we have heard these executives talk about how someone told them, "Start learning about people as people." Then they practiced, practiced, and practiced. If they practiced at least 15 times, they may have formed a habit. After a while, they probably found that developing relationships had gotten a great deal easier, and their new results positively reinforced the reasons for developing powerful business relationships.

Finally, in our interviews, we found that many relationship experts reinforce a connection or thank people with handwritten notes. As Doug Renfro, president of Renfro Foods, Inc., says, "I send everyone a hand-written thank-you note. People love hand-written notes. It means a lot more than e-mail."[9] And Tom Feeney, president and CEO of Safelite Group, Inc., parent company of Safelite AutoGlass, told us something similar when he said:

I write hand-written notes to genuinely thank someone for their time, but I also believe it distinguishes me from others. It is not an e-mail. I think it is easier to send an e-mail. Since it is perceived as harder to do this, people recognize that it is unique. I've had people say back to me, "Hey, I got your note. That was really nice to see a hand-written note; we don't get those anymore." It is always good to deliver the unexpected . . . whether it is to associates, customers, or clients.[10]

In these digital times, sometimes the most primitive technology can help to humanize your connections with customers and others. We live in a world where things can be done in nanoseconds. As a result, we often feel compelled to move quickly, focused on task. In our experience, though, and in the experience of many relationship experts, people need relationships to get and keep them energized. Connecting first can help to energize someone to take the next step, whatever it might be.

In addition to developing individual practices, some companies select talented people who already have the ability to connect and build that practice into their cultures. At Southwest Airlines, the boundary spanner—the employee who is responsible for coordinating the 11 people so as to get fast turnaround times for aircraft—has been carefully selected as someone who can connect and coordinate. Southwest is an organization known for hiring former school teachers and performers as flight attendants because they have experience at connecting with their audience. This selection has partially led to the fastest turnaround times in the airline industry.

TEAM

As a service provider, *Southwest understands that for customers to feel good about their experience, the company's employees must relate or connect with them.* How did the people in that role develop the individual and team skills necessary to coordinate 11 other people, including a number of people high above them in the organizational chart? The boundary spanner and all the other people on the takeoff team—indeed, all the employees at Southwest—have been screened for relational competence, one of Southwest's paramount hiring criteria.

Daniel Hanson, author of *Cultivating Common Ground: Releasing the Power of Relationships at Work,* shows what can happen in a culture that values "relationship competence" by saying:

> Environments in which people confirm each other are full of a special power. It is a power that emerges from people who feel good about themselves and receive energy from connecting to

others. It is a power that the people who care for their work and each other know from firsthand experience. On the other side of the coin, environments in which people are encouraged to look out for themselves or taught to be selective about who they care for stifle the human spirit. In the short run, these environments can produce results, but over the long haul, they suffer from a lack of community spirit. They are deprived of the power of relationships. Indeed, they often suffer as a result of negative energy that draws people's attention, thus their energy, away from their work and each other.[11]

The Importance of Connecting with a Customer

Bruce Barnes, former Fortune 100 Chief Information Officer (CIO) and current faculty member at The Ohio State University, wanted suppliers to know that in order to connect with him, they first had to understand what he was looking for. For Barnes:

Top-tier IT [information technology] leaders play to a bigger purpose. We are (or should be) well beyond the point where it's myopically all about the costs. In truth it's instead all about value. What will I quantifiably get from this, as opposed to simply being focused on minimizing the initial cost of entry? What's going to actually come of it, and how will I unambiguously know its goal has been achieved? I'm thinking about numerators . . . top line; I'm thinking far less about denominators . . . bottom-line costs.

Salespeople that come to me need to realize that an end-of-the-quarter deal is meaningless unless the result of that acquisition will yield quantifiable improvements to my company's ultimate bottom line . . . as the company measures it. That requires an educated provider, or you are wasting my time.

Along those lines, I feel it is appropriate to set expectations early, so as to avoid wasting people's valuable time. To those quota-motivated sales folks, I always begin by telling them that their job is not to sell me anything. To their expected shock and dismay, I often say, "Look at my phone. There are . . . three business cards right here next to my phone. See them? Do you know who they are?"

In response to the confused looks, I say, "These are my trusted advisors." We have developed a relationship of mutual trust and confidence. We have arrived at a point of mutual respect and shared knowledge, whereby they are looking out for me and vice versa. I always keep them close and will always call them first when I am faced with an issue, and it is only three because that minimizes the complexity in my life.

I then say, "Your job isn't to sell me anything. Your job is to figure out how to get to the point where you become one of those three cards. It's a far different game, and it will require more effort on your part. You are not a salesperson with me. You are instead here to try to establish a trusted value-based, content-rich relationship with me. Ultimately, if you are successful in becoming one of those three cards, your reward is that I will keep you informed and engaged in all that I do; otherwise, I may likely ignore you, or at least relegate this relationship to others in my group that only care about cost, where your tenure will only be as long as you are the cheapest. That's the deal . . . you can choose to play or not."[12]

Long-term, profitable relationships don't take place simply by selling products or services but by connecting and delivering value over time. The deal is not to sell stuff or to create a relationship that Barnes has to spend time managing. As he says, "The real deal is to become a 'trusted advisor.'"[13] Barnes says that he regularly told salespeople this, but only a few salespeople were tenacious enough to become one of the three cards. Those few, however, were the ones Barnes really wanted to connect with anyway.

Some Customers Expect Deeper Connections

Some customers expect deeper relationships with their critical suppliers, especially if they are highly dependent on them. While we may appreciate the people who keep our office plants thriving, we are not dependent on them for getting our business results. On the other hand, we often need a strong relationship with our technology providers. The degree of interdependence elevates the relationship stakes. When we decide to connect first, we have made the decision to invest in that relationship in order to get better results. In the customer- and technical-service arenas, for example, connecting first is critical, but these days, as we have seen, this need to connect is too often overlooked or seen as a waste of money.

Is there a person out there who has not spent considerable money on some product or service and ended up cursing after having to wade through an unresponsive computerized "help desk"? It seems an almost universal occurrence to find oneself in some sort of digital loop, which ends up taking you back to menus that offered no help the first time.

Worse yet, after having searched for a response for 15 minutes, is realizing that the help system has hung up on you. These kinds of situations are why swear words were invented. Firms that provide their customers with real people who can connect with them first and then solve the problem can differentiate themselves in a hurry. They realize that this connecting yields better business results. Connecting first with the customer also can give suppliers insights into their business that they could not have gotten just by analyzing call statistics.

Zappos, a brand almost synonymous with exceptional customer service,[14] started by selling shoes online. It is now a $1 billion per year retailer. Tony Hsieh, Zappos' CEO, says that the company made many decisions early on that led to a strong customer-focused culture. Some of the most notable of them were

>> Encouraging customers to order as many products as they wanted in order to "try them" as well as offering free return shipping for a full 365 days.
>> Encouraging customers to call the company about nearly everything. The company's call center takes 5,000 calls per

day, and employees work independent of scripts, quotas, or call time limits. The longest call to date has been four hours. Zappos views the phone experience as a branding device and speaks to virtually every customer at least once.[15]

Inc. Magazine cited an example regarding a woman who called Zappos to return a pair of boots for her husband because he died in a car accident. The next day, she received a flower delivery, which the call center rep had billed to the company without checking with her supervisor.[16] The company's stellar customer-focused culture has led Zappos to become an e-commerce juggernaut and a case study for many businesses and business schools. It is rare to see such strong customer connections being made when companies are competing on prices and where the customer-service rep is measured by the average call time per customer rather than on meeting customers' needs.

Conclusion

Taking time to invest in a relationship is usually a great use of time! Connecting before task allows people to be acknowledged and listened to, perhaps the highest compliment we can pay in our culture. However, if the acknowledgment is insincere (the telemarketer asking, "How are you?" before asking for money), we can sense this quickly and hang up, literally and figuratively.

If the person initiating the connection is sincere in her efforts to learn about us, though, we respond because we like talking about ourselves—and so few people really want to know about us. If this recognition and caring predominate in a corporate culture, the energy and creativity generated become a differentiator. We said earlier that we believe that relationship energy remains one of the best ways to make an exponential leap in productivity and stock price.

POINTS TO REMEMBER

Overview

>> Some call it small talk, but in many ways connecting first is the lifeblood of business. It is not about manipulation or just exchanging pleasantries for the sake of it, but genuinely making an effort to find a way to relate and share a common ground before moving straight to accomplishing the task at hand.

>> Failure to connect first can slow us down; lead us to a waste of time, resources, and costs; and lead us or others to be physically present but mentally absent at work.

 ## For Individuals

>> It is especially important to connect when
  ○ Working with people who you don't know well
  ○ The topic at hand is likely to be sensitive or contentious
  ○ Something seems off but has not been identified or discussed
  ○ A problem needs to be resolved

>> Benefits of connecting first in business relationships:
  ○ Deciding the extent to which to invest in building a relationship
  ○ Being able to better understand how the other person thinks and what he or she values
  ○ Sharing common ground and trust to enable faster problem solving
  ○ Building a comfortable rapport, thereby earning you the opportunity to ask for business in the future

>> In customer- and technical-service arenas, connecting first is especially crucial to strengthening the customer relationship with the brand and thereby gaining a sustainable competitive advantage.

For Teams

>> Connecting first can enable teams to identify potential barriers and obstacles at the offset, preventing larger issues or delays down the road.

>> Think of a time when you sensed something was "off" with a team member, but you weren't able to pinpoint it. Could connecting first have revealed the underlying issue?

>> Personalities, preferences, and styles vary greatly from person to person. How can connecting first affect the way you cater your communication style to team members?

For Organizations

>> How does the culture within your organization affect the way you communicate with your team? Does a "get to work" mentality prevent you from properly connecting with coworkers first?

>> Some companies understand that customers must connect with company employees on a personal level in order to feel good about their experience. How much of an effort does your company make to connect with its customers (both in availability and tone)?

NOTES

_____

_____

_____

_____

_____

_____

_____

_____

KEY #2

Learn by Walking in Another's Shoes

Bill Joe Shaver, a Texas country singer, wrote and recorded a ballad entitled, "I Couldn't Be Me Without You." At least one of the reasons the song is a classic is that the message is universal. Others can refine and complete us. They can bring out the best—or, sadly, the worst—in us. Although we might not have had such a relationship with another person, the broader message is that we cannot thrive in business or life without relating to others. Like it or not, we need one another to become fully human. In a very real sense, I couldn't be me without you.

To be involved in a healthy relationship means that we feel connected, understood, and valued. This is why our first key was *connect first*. As an extension of connecting with one another, we can begin to understand what it is like to walk in another's shoes. Thus we know that we are not alone because someone else can imagine, in a more detached manner, *what it feels like to be me*. That is, they can imagine what it might be like *to walk in my shoes*.

In our highly competitive business world, where independence and self-sufficiency are often rewarded, this desire for empathy may seem counterintuitive. In fact, some of you may be thinking: who cares how my business colleague feels? I have enough to worry about just taking care of myself and my job. I don't have time to worry about how others feel!

We would submit, however, that by being focused only on your own work and not taking time to understand how colleagues feel is actually *slowing you down and significantly limiting your influence*. Why is that? To have little empathy means that you are focused primarily on yourself. Who wants to listen to, help, or work with someone who is self-centered? How can you trust a person if he or she sincerely doesn't care about others? Because relationships are built on social exchange, when there is no empathy, the relationship is one-sided, out of whack.

The Dynamics of a Social Exchange

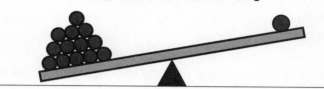

Being able to empathize with others when trying to forge or deepen a relationship or when trying to solve a problem can help you in several ways:

>> Because you can imagine what it might be like to walk in another's shoes, *you can adapt your problem-solving approach to get the best results* for everyone. If your colleague needs to understand the big picture first, you can start with that. If another member of your team needs to understand first why something is important, you can start with that. And so it goes.

>> In turn, because *you are empathic and more adaptable, people will find you easier to work with*. Thus they may be more willing to consider how what they do might affect you.

>> By first walking in another's shoes, *you can anticipate possible problems*, saving both parties time and hassle. For example, we could ask Samantha, "If we moved your department to another floor, how might this affect your team?" By knowing the answer to questions such as this, you can avoid rework.

>> Finally, *being empathic will increase your ability to influence others because you will learn over time what works and what doesn't in your relationships*. It will increase your self-awareness and make you more effective. This, in turn, will give you more personal power.

Jack Fish, a former executive of GlaxoSmithKline (US) and now an S4 Consulting practice leader, explains how this works in business:

> I believe that having solid relationships should be a core business competency. You have to thoroughly understand your own business and at the same time know how your business partners operate, their expertise, and the areas where you can work together to help each other grow. Transparency will help the process move quickly when you find common ground. Looking for new opportunities is not doing the old things better. Taking risk together is a smart, calculated, thoughtful way that drives the enterprising spirit. When done right, these efforts create the energy to move forward in trusting, productive, and lasting relationships.[1]

In face-to-face or phone conversations, it is easier to walk in another's shoes and understand our impact on others. In virtual communications, however, it is much more difficult and sometimes almost impossible. Sadly, sometimes we *even seem to forget that there is a person,* another human being, on the other side of the screen. Although technology enables us to share information more quickly, it can also pressure us to focus more on task than on relationship, often making the uniqueness of others invisible. Other people, departments, or companies simply become the next step in some process we need to complete. For example, we "use" others to provide input into a report, review a work product, secure travel arrangements for us, and so on. *Whether we mean to or not, we can be in such a hurry that others can become simply cogs in the wheel of business.* It's not surprising, then, that far too many people go home at the end of the day exhausted and drained, feeling as though no one really knows or cares who they are.

Do you see coworkers as people—or as a means to accomplish specific tasks?

If we are going to thrive as individuals, departments, and companies, people need to feel understood and appreciated. We need to feel as though others can imagine what our world is like. When others care about and value us, we are energized and renewed. How is your energy level at the end of each day? Are you energized and renewed, or are you exhausted? If it's the latter, then some of the practices in this chapter may be of help.

It's the Little Things that Wear Us Down

Gloria, a woman from the finance department, was responsible for compiling the company's annual budget. Every year this required getting all department heads to submit their departmental budgets by a certain date. For years, prior to the due date, Gloria had sent numerous e-mails reminding people of the impending date. In meetings with those same department heads, she had repeatedly explained the importance of getting their budgets in on time. Yet some of the department heads always turned their budgets in late. Her boss would not permit her to issue false deadlines, so she began to resent some of her colleagues, and this resentment had leaked onto other interactions as well.

Over time, relationships on the leadership team became more strained. Finally, the friction on the team came to a head. When trying to sort out some of the underlying concerns, the budget issue arose. Gloria minced no words when sharing her growing frustration. The team was taken aback about the degree of her frustration. When asked about the impact of their delay on her, she explained that it had meant that she had to work several weekends to complete the budget. One of those weekends was always around— sometimes on—her youngest son's birthday. The department heads knew that she was a single mother, but they *had no idea* the sacrifice she was making because they were late. They were embarrassed and dismayed about their impact on their colleague. For as many years as they had worked together, they never really knew— or appreciated—the true cost of missing their deadline.

On the other hand, Gloria also didn't fully appreciate why some department heads were always late. In discussion, they confessed that they put off preparing their budgets because they did not know how to pull them together, especially for some cross-functional projects. Because they were not "financial types," they dreaded creating their budgets and were embarrassed to ask for help. When their conversation ended, the department heads had learned something about the unintended consequences of waiting to ask for help, and the finance person had learned who needed help in developing their budgets. Together the leadership team learned how to value and support each other. This enabled them to turn a dreaded event—creating the annual budget—into an opportunity to work together and learn from one another.

What Empathy Looks Like

In *To Kill a Mockingbird*, Scout Finch is trying to make sense of the people around her, especially people like Boo Radley, a very private and rather odd neighbor who hides little trinkets for Scout and her brother in a tree. As her father Atticus, a wise small-town Southern lawyer, tells her:

> If you can learn a simple trick ... you'll get along better with all kinds of folks. You never really understand a person until you consider things from his point of view, until you climb into his skin and walk around in it.[2]

In one of the final scenes of the movie version, we watch Scout walking Boo Radley down the block and across his porch to the front door of his house, hand in hand. He has saved her life, and their relationship has taught her something profound—Atticus was right—*you can't really know someone until you have walked in their shoes.* As Boo steps into his house and closes the door, we see Scout retracing Boo's steps across the porch, slowly stepping into each footstep. Now she has begun to understand him and the gifts this relationship brings.

This empathy is profoundly different from sympathy. Sympathy is the emotion we feel when we are sorry for someone. Sometimes sympathy can make us feel a little above the other, too. Like it or not, we're sometimes glad we're not in their shoes. Empathy, on the other hand, is attempting to *feel what the other person might be feeling*. It is about being equal with the other person—understanding the world from his or her point of view. It does not mean agreeing with the person; rather, it's a matter of simply trying to experience what the person may be feeling. It is one place where we begin to connect with another.

Operation Bear Hug: Empathy in Business-to-Business Relationships by IBM

When Lou Gerstner became IBM's CEO in 1993, he created Operation Bear Hug, a massive empathy program that required the company's top 50 managers to visit at least five of the company's biggest customers in just three months. The managers were not asked to go to the customers to sell products and services. Their task was to just listen, yes, you read that right . . . simply listen to customers' concerns and think about how IBM could help. These executives' 200 direct reports then had to do the same.

This helped managers to hear the customers' concerns first-hand and see whether a particular decision added value for them or not. In the process, the managers discovered some major oppor-tunities as well. For example, managers found that large corporate clients were enamored of the web but confused about how to use it effectively. IBM realized that it could provide the infrastructure needed to help these corporations to fully use the power of the web. This resulted in IBM's e-business initiative, which was not just successful but also paved the way for the company's long-term growth.

**By giving customers the microphone, businesses are able
to see problems from a different perspective.**

When the program was started, some felt it was foolish to use the top executives' time when they could have been concentrating on getting more customers by just selling products. But Operation Bear Hug led to quicker actions to resolve customer problems as well as stronger long-term customer relationships. The company's dramatic turnaround and successful entry into professional services further proves the point. Today, a routine visit to *listen* to customers is common at IBM.

This extreme customer focus engrained in the company by Lou Gerstner led it to a "decade of uninterrupted double-digit revenue and earnings growth"[3] and made the managers a lot more comfortable in taking on new challenges.

Practicing empathy requires us to identify with the needs and expectations of others—be it people, other teams, or other businesses. Those who are known for their ability to develop and grow business relationships practice empathy daily. They also tend to be extremely successful. Rob Bennett, former president and CEO of

Nova Scotia Power, Inc., Halifax, Nova Scotia, and currently executive vice president and chief operations officer (COO) of Emera, is one of these people. Bennett is widely known for his deep technical knowledge, his ability to generate highly innovative solutions to complex strategic opportunities, and his exceptional ability to nurture and foster relationships. Given that skill set, it is no wonder that he and his teams have produced outstanding results.

Interestingly, what lies behinds Bennett's exceptional ability to nurture and foster relationships *and* his ability to generate strategic innovations (these are interconnected) is his ability to empathize. Nova Scotia is known for its rugged, spectacularly beautiful landscape—and for its challenging weather. Strong storms make power reliability a challenge both for power producers and for customers. If you want to see empathy in action, watch Bennett when a strong storm roars in and takes out the generators that control the hydroelectric dam. After the engineers and reporters have left the site, and in the faint morning light so that no one will notice him, you will catch Rob Bennett walking alone across the top of the dam. In part, he is revisiting the technical challenge and proposed solution—and in part, he is walking across the dam to viscerally know what it would mean for the community below if power could not be restored in a timely manner. He is walking in his customers' shoes and reminding himself that his company has to move quickly. What happens to these people profoundly matters to him.

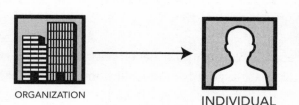

By walking in their customers' shoes, leaders can better assess the impact of decisions.

ORGANIZATION

INDIVIDUAL

If you want to learn how Bennett generates such innovative strategic solutions, ask him to replay his thought process for a green energy solution. What you'll hear is how he thinks through the concerns of and impact on each of the stakeholders, customers, regulators, provincial leaders, First Nations, and the shareholders of his company. Systematically, he walks in the shoes of each and tries to see what Emera can do to help all the stakeholders succeed. Although he is strongly committed to the success of Emera, Bennett's concern for and commitment to creating win-win solutions whenever possible is what underlies both his positional and personal power.

What It's Like to Not Have Empathy

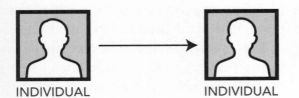

INDIVIDUAL   INDIVIDUAL

Jason's inability to connect makes his interpersonal relationships a one-way street.

Although people like Rob Bennett have a deep ability to empathize, some struggle mightily because of their lack of empathy. Jason is a 15-year-old boy with Asperger's syndrome, one of whose symptoms is a greatly lessened sense of empathy. He cannot quickly establish human contact because in most cases he does not see the other person whole. He cannot imagine what it is like to walk in that person's shoes. He is preoccupied with getting only his needs met. Because of this, relationships are difficult for Jason. He misses verbal and physical cues, so interactions are awkward. In many cases this forces him to swim alone and often against the current in a sea of relationships.

As you can see, recognizing only your needs puts you at a major disadvantage when you are trying to build relationships that can bring out the best in both parties. Why? Because you can't connect with another person unless you care enough to imagine what it's like to be that person. This is the reason it is so important to connect with the people you work for and with *first*. A connection enables you to see the world from their perspective and allows you to better understand the lens through which they view the world.

Boosting Employee Loyalty Through Layoffs at RainSoft

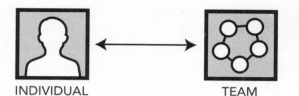

INDIVIDUAL   TEAM

Relationships need to be built between executives and the teams they lead.

Frank Kneller, CEO of RainSoft, had a tough decision in front of him in late 2008; he knew that he would have to lay off 25 percent of his workforce. But rather than going ahead with it, he chose to wait until after the Christmas holiday to lay off workers. The board of directors was not happy with this decision, but he chose to stick by it.

Having communicated with the employees at monthly town hall meetings about the economic condition of the company, he personally made the announcement to them about the layoffs. At the meeting that followed, "he was visibly upset, even cr[ied] as he hugged an employee who'd lost her job," and he even apologized to the other laid-off employees. Unlike other organizations, he made sure that the laid-off employees had computer access as long as they were around and had enough time to clear their desks and talk to their friends rather than be walked out the door immediately. This empathetic corporate CEO did something few CEOs and executives would do. Kneller's behavior during this time went a long way in giving him and RainSoft a loyalty boost. As one of his production-planning employees puts it, "It's a breath of fresh air when a CEO is out there in front of everybody and shows [that] he actually cares. In general, people are more loyal now." Another employee, Edith, said, "We see that he cares, and we try to work with him."[4]

Working with Those Who Think Differently

With people who are very much like us, empathy is easy. If you are from the same town or city and you've lived in the same place all along, everybody knows how things work. Empathy is also easy in a confined environment where the traditions are set. It's easier to read cues and to make accurate assumptions about what they mean. In this global business world, though, with its interconnected cultures, firms, and supply chains, our assumptions about what certain behaviors mean can easily get us into big trouble.

When we start working with people who think differently, who see the world differently, and who have different habits, we have to work at developing empathy if we want to relate and get work done efficiently and effectively. We have to learn more about their culture if we want to understand what it might be like to walk in their shoes. In many cases, this adjustment is not an easy task, but it is critical for business success.

We don't have to think of cross-cultural business relationships to fully understand this. For example, many technical people tend to work best with other technical people. Their world is logical and orderly. But when they start dealing with nontechnical people, they often become frustrated by the different ways these nontechnical people think and work. Technical folks often find their nontechnical colleagues' approaches not only inefficient but also ineffective. The nontechnical colleagues may find their technical colleagues too focused on the task or too limited in their view. In many cases it's not a matter of who's right and who's wrong but rather a matter of how can we better understand what it's like to be in the other peoples' heads so that we can adapt, bridge our differences, and arrive at the best solution.

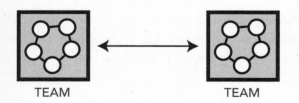

Teams who can understand the needs and goals of others have a better chance to unleash powerful relationships within their organization.

Being more empathetic with those not like us can allow us to complement rather than frustrate one another. We saw this in spades when we were working with a manufacturing company to resolve major production issues. As part of the process, we led the leadership team through alignment sessions that specifically promoted cross-functional communication. In this company, there was a fairly common clash between two departments. The following exchange between the heads of the operations and sales departments highlights this type of problem:

Mark, the head of sales, began by saying to Juan, the head of operations, "You don't care about the hard work we do and the revenue we generate. We are bringing you all these dream deals. We're breaking our backs trying to grow this business, and all you ever do is complain about the new business."

"Listen," said Juan, "When you bring me *your* dream deal, it's almost *never a dream for us* because your dream deal almost always requires us to do extra and unplanned work. Your dream deal is full of bells and whistles, many of which you forget to tell us about. That lack of communication and nonplanned work mean that we are going to blow our budget and be penalized. In too many cases you've made promises that we can't possibly meet, so we are going to be penalized for that, too. We are going to have to work a lot of overtime. Other projects are going to have to be put on hold. *Your dream deal is often our worst nightmare*! It's not that I don't want to help you and grow the business. I absolutely do, but you give us information about your dream deal so far down the line that there is no way we can do it!"

"I never realized that," said Mark.

"No," said Juan, "because you never took the time to come talk to me—to us—*before* you agreed to the deal. *Together* we could have created a real dream deal. Instead, you just threw it over the wall and said, 'Go to it.'"

"Well," said the president, who was watching the whole exchange, "Now you can work differently together in the future. So how do you two propose to turn our opportunity with Global Fixtures into a dream deal so that we can avoid future production problems and become more effective and profitable?"

Empathy within the World of Differing Cultures

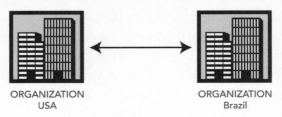

ORGANIZATION
USA

ORGANIZATION
Brazil

Let's take something fairly simple. Your company's headquarters are located in the United States of America, and you are assigned to work on two projects, one in Japan and one in Brazil. Your job is to create the agenda and lead the kick-off meetings for both projects. Do you know what it is like to walk in the shoes of Japanese or Brazilian businesspeople? If not, and you follow the typical American business format of going straight to task, your projects will likely get off to a rocky start—although you might not realize it immediately. There are rituals in both countries as to how business relationships begin and how you show respect. Without this knowledge, you're flying blind about how to connect with your global partners.

Many executives work with foreign cultures and as a result are faced with the challenge of establishing rapport and empathy with partners who not only do not speak their language but in some cases live in what are now considered preindustrial societies.

Nicholas Wolfson, a colleague, faced this when working in Mauritania early in his career a number of years ago. Wolfson, a master at developing productive and powerful relationships, describes how he first learned the importance of understanding and empathizing with other cultures in his Peace Corps experience in Mauritania:

> I was dealing with people who were so different from me that I needed to find a common ground before I could even talk about the project that I was there to work on. There needed to be a place where I could "see" them and they could "see" me in order to be able to start a conversation—build a relationship—to accomplish the work we might do together.

We didn't have a common language. That is, they spoke Hassaniyya, and I spoke English and French. I came from a modern mechanized society, while they came from a society in which basically nothing had changed since long before the birth of Christ. In developing societies, the whole point is to not change anything. For them, today needs to be exactly like yesterday—innovation is viewed as the enemy. Any kind of change is a threat to the existence of the social system and the people in it. I had been asked to help a people who feel—not without reason—that any change is bad.[5]

Wolfson described his approach to empathy by saying

So, I'm looking for a common ground. First, our group let the others literally "see" us, watch us from a distance. Rather than roar up to a settlement and startle them, we decided to settle far enough away for them to observe us, but not be afraid of us. We set up our cots and just hung out for a while reading books and doing chores, so they could see what we were like, what we were up to. After a few hours, they wandered over to meet us.

In that culture, the common ground ended up at least in the beginning being politeness, consideration, smiling, knowing the greetings. That was the fundamental social grease that kept them comfortable. So I remembered what somebody told us in training: honor their rituals and their culture. Do what they do. If somebody gives you three cups of tea, whether you want them or not, take them. Slurp the tea; it's polite in that culture. It's showing that you are enjoying it. Slurp and take all three cups; do not ever turn them down; don't ever say, "No I don't want tea." *Because it is not about your desires; it's about your demonstrating respect and appreciation.* It's about learning to understand what it is like to walk in their shoes. Do that first. It's a way of gaining mileage, and you need all the mileage you can get in cross-cultural work.[6]

Cultivating Emptiness:
An Approach to Empathy

Joan Holmes, founding president of The Hunger Project, describes her own foreign experiences in developing empathy this way:

> Working cross-culturally was exciting to me. It was a challenge. For example, when I was in Africa, the head of the African division introduced me by saying, "Please ignore her skin color; she is African at heart." And in some ways I was. When I was in Africa, I felt African. And when I was in Bangladesh, the people said, "Oh, she is emotional like we are in Bangladesh; she is a Bangladeshi." When I was in India, I was Indian. Working cross-culturally with those relationships—I loved doing that, and I was eager to know how that culture worked and eager to be in a relationship with the people of that culture without imposing anything from my own culture. I was trying to learn theirs. And to develop a relationship that was so powerful cross-culturally that it could be productive toward achieving the common vision of eliminating hunger.[7]

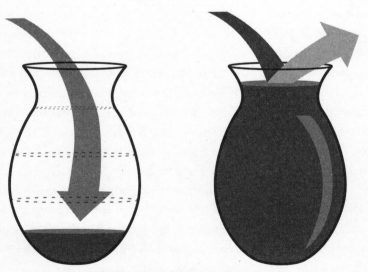

To empathize, we seek to become empty vessels so as to be
filled by understanding another's experience.

People who are particularly empathetic are often able to become almost an empty vessel, ready to be filled by the person with whom a connection is desired. They come into relationships selflessly, open to the other person, wanting to know what it might be like to be that person. It's a rare but critical skill. Too often our first response, especially in business, is to move the focus from the person back to us as we share a similar experience that happened to us.

Dr. Peter Goldsmith, the highly respected scholar, consultant, and entrepreneur in global management and agribusiness we mentioned earlier, is particularly adept at working with different cultures. He demonstrates Holmes' point about the necessity of getting outside one's head by describing himself in what most of us would call a selling situation. He told us:

> I'm going to go into a meeting at 11:00 a.m. with multi-nationalists who work in Argentina. In that case (and it's the same anywhere I work in the world) I am just going in only to understand their problem and point of view. I won't be selling anything, nor talking about myself, I'm just trying to understand their problem and why it is so important to them. Sometimes I'll provide analytical support, but the purpose of the meeting is really just to understand what they are struggling with and share possible ideas. They then—if they think our time together was worthwhile—may decide to partner on some research or some project. I think relationship begins with a lot of selfless discussion, walking in each other's shoes. If you start there and do good work, good things will happen. It's very helpful to be able to step back, just listen, and let stuff roll over you.[8]

Caring at the Heart of It All

Empathy is at the heart of caring and appreciation. Unless we have a deep sense of who the other person is, it is far too easy to ignore his or her interests or to make that person a mere step in a process.

What must one do to practice caring and empathy? As Nicholas Wolfson says:

You have to be really interested. *You have to want to know.* You really have to generate caring for the person that you are talking with. You don't have to say, "I love you," but you do have to care. And it is all in that domain of being willing to love your fellow human being. You are reaching out to people. You make it your business to connect. It could be the waiter who comes over when you are having lunch; connect with the waiter. Don't deal with him like he is a piece of machinery—like he is a gas pump or something. Connect with them.[9]

Whether you run a global business or an organization with a global mission to end hunger, you have to generate caring and you have to connect—really connect—with hundreds of people in dozens of cultures. Joan Holmes here tells us of how she sees meeting those people who might move her project along, saying:

If someone came up to me, I was always authentically thrilled to meet the person because I saw that person as a part of the constituency to end hunger. So no matter who I met, I wanted to get to know them better and let them know about our vision. When you meet someone—if you meet them at a concert, for example, you know they like music, and so you have something in common. So I endeavor to find a place, a space, of shared interest. It may not be The Hunger Project yet, but a shared interest based on little clues that were available at that time.[10]

Toro's New Empathetic Approach Reduces Lawsuits

In the late 1980s, Toro, a premier maker of lawnmowers, was struggling because of lawsuits for over 100 serious accidents a year filed by its customers. In the middle of all these problems, Toro brought in a new CEO, Ken Melrose. Because Melrose was empathetic with customers, he was able to reduce the number and subsequent cost of the lawsuits.

Ken Melrose started sending a company representative to meet with the injured person and his or her family to see what went wrong, sympathize with them, and offer any assistance they needed in recovering from the accident. Before this change, half the injuries resulted in a lawsuit. Because Melrose installed empathy as part of the Toro culture, that number dropped to only *one lawsuit* since 1991.[11]

This is the power of recognition, of listening, of caring, and of empathy.

The Power of Empathy

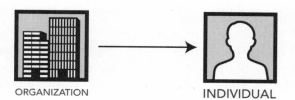

ORGANIZATION   INDIVIDUAL

To be seen as empathetic by the customer, companies have to first be empathetic to their people.

In the Tampa airport once we witnessed how Southwest Airlines practiced empathy—both for customers and for a company employee—and how powerfully the practice worked. We were getting ready to board a plane, and the gate agent informed us that we were waiting for one flight attendant who had just gotten an important telephone call. So the agent said, "We'll board as soon as she gets here." When the attendant approached the gate area, she was sobbing. Another Southwest representative stepped in, listened to her carefully, gave her a hug, and sent her on her way. Although everyone had witnessed this scene, the gate agent got on the speaker and calmly said, "We've been waiting for the flight attendant to get here, but we've just found out that a member of her family has been in a very serious automobile accident. She really needs to go be with them. I'm sure you can all imagine what that would feel like. So we're going to ask you to be patient while we find another flight attendant. If you want to sit back down and relax, we'll keep you informed. We think it is going to take us about 20 minutes. At this point we do not expect this will impact any of your connection times. Thank you."

The Southwest employee had said—very pointedly—"I'm sure you all can imagine what this feels like." He wanted us to empathize with the flight attendant. *Because we could empathize with her, we could adjust our expectations and not be resentful.* Not only had we empathized with her, but the Southwest agent had empathized with us in our concerns about a delay. True to the agent's word, the new flight attendant arrived 20 minutes later, and the plane made up the time in the air so that no connections were missed. The experience was handled so professionally that whenever we see that gate in the Tampa airport, we remember that situation and once again appreciate how Southwest cared for both its attendant and its customers.

There are many examples of how being empathic can lead to higher levels of productivity and profit. Bruce Barnes, former Fortune 100 chief information officer (CIO) and current faculty member at The Ohio State University, believes that empathy is critical to the human connection:

> When I talk about the importance of empathy, I'm really talking about understanding the mental model(s) of the person/people across the table from you. What do they value, and how do they see things? Are you effectively dialing into what is really going on in the six inches between their ears? Become your customer! If I am not resonating with their perspective and their motivations, no matter how much sense I think I'm making, I'm not effectively making my point and, in effect, [am] speaking in a foreign language that will be dismissed. You absolutely need to speak to other parties in a way that is both meaningful and personal to them, in a language that they understand, appreciate, and value. An easy concept, perhaps; however, that takes ongoing work, preparation, and discipline to be skilled in doing it.[12]

Jim Hallett, CEO of KAR Auction Services, Inc., says:

I think empathy enables me to relate to that person in a way that I can draw certain comparisons to my own life. Maybe I try to understand how that person thinks. When that person tells me something about his life that I find interesting, I wonder what that would be like. I wonder what it would be like having your dad having to work a second job to pay for your education. I wonder what it would be like working in the steel mill all day, sweating. You see these guys in the steel mill and those hot furnaces. I actually see those visions. I wonder what that would be like. Doing this helps me understand their world and allows me to work with them more effectively.[13]

Others draw on empathy to understand expectations and build the foundation for a customer or supplier relationship. Jeff Schwantz, a 15+ year business-to-business relationship manager, always asks questions in the first meeting that few others do:

"How do you want to work together? And tell me what could I do that would just really anger you?" Anytime I start working with a firm now, that's one of my questions that I ask right up front. "What could I do to put this relationship so far in the ditch, what would that be?"[14]

It seems a dangerous question to ask, but Schwantz says it gets an almost immediate reply, describing behavior that the executive feels would end the relationship. Schwantz wants to know the executive's highest expectations so that he can create systems and processes to meet them.

Tom Feeney, president and CEO of Safelite Group, Inc., parent company of Safelite AutoGlass, started out wanting to be a chief financial officer (CFO). Now he is viewed more as a talented leader and a masterful relationship builder; he leads an enormously successful business. Feeney explains that it was an indirect route that took him to an understanding of how to harness the value in business relationships. As he says:

> *It wasn't until I got into operations, then moved into sales and went out to meet customers directly, that I understood relationships can produce economic value.* When I was selected to run a business selling mufflers and brakes in Chicago, I found the previous management had taken the royalty checks and kept the franchisees at bay. My approach was "our business will be better off the more the franchisees contributed to the strategy and the direction of the business." These are the individuals who are facing our customers everyday, and if we listen to them more, the company will be more successful.
>
> I would invite them in and ask what their needs were, where we could help them. I wanted to really understand their world. I believed that the more successful they were, the more successful we'd be because we'd get higher royalties. And it worked out that way—whether it was modifications to the advertising plan or helping them in negotiating lower prices with a supplier—all of the purchases they would make for mufflers or brakes or shocks. So we helped them lower their product cost, which made them more profitable, which allowed them to open more stores and drive our revenues as well. That probably was my first inclination about openness, building relationships, understanding other people's needs, and solving those needs to the benefit of yourself and your business.[15]

Feeney came from the more analytical, left-brained world, but came to realize that relationships, requiring more right-brain skills, were not "soft" things. He saw that acting in a hands-off manner with the franchisees would limit his firm's growth and profit potential. There are some finance people who do not truly understand about the necessity of maintaining relationships, but Tom Feeney listened to the franchisees, and they grew together.

Traditional Contracting and Empathy: Esso/ITNet

The most effective leaders, when trying to solve problems, often think about what it's like to be their customer or their supplier. You can see this most easily in certain kinds of negotiations. One of the major foundational skills in planning for a negotiation is to understand the interests and needs of the other party. And the more empathetic you can be—the more you can put yourself in that person's shoes—the more possible it is to come out with a creative win-win solution.

When there is a lack of empathy, the cost can sometimes be high. In their book, *The Relationship Advantage: Information Technologies, Sourcing, and Management*, Thomas Kern and Leslie P. Willcocks studied hundreds of information technology (IT) outsourcing engagements. They present the 1994 example of Esso UK, a huge energy company, and ITNet, an IT outsourcing supplier. Esso UK wanted to outsource part of its IT function for five years. ITNet won the $2 million bid and started working with Esso UK. Esso UK had never outsourced its IT before. This led to problems from the beginning of the contract. As Willcocks says:

> Esso's clarity about both objectives ... and detail[s] of the contract focused on the arrangements but [was not enough to] ... ensure relational effectiveness. Consequently, the first few years were riddled with operational difficulties, especially for the supplier, whose erroneous bid calculations caused serious service-level problems and relational pressures, eventually leading to ... loggerheads and an over-reliance on the contract.[16]

By saying "an over-reliance on the contract," Willcocks meant that Esso UK started treating ITNet adversarially, focusing more and more on the letter of the contract, as the company usually did with suppliers. The company saw this as a smart, hard-headed business practice. But there were terms in the contract that could easily have ended the relationship. For example, the contract specified that ITNet would provide upgrades to all the software Esso UK was using. The difficulty was that if ITNet bought and installed each new generation of software, a time-consuming process, it would lack the resources to hit the service targets specified by Esso, and ITNet would lose a great deal of money on the deal. The difficulty for Esso UK was that if it dropped ITNet, it would have to start the outsourcing over and would have to spend hundreds of thousands of dollars in changeover costs.

Both firms analyzed their situation, and they arrived at similar conclusions. Neither ITNet nor Esso UK had developed and built in the relationship-oriented capabilities and skills that would have developed empathy, trust, risk mitigation, and effective project processes. They had not built the powerful business relationships that both needed. The Esso UK–ITNet relationship improved when ITNet and Esso UK both created supplier relationship-management roles: two people—one from each firm—primarily interested in helping to ensure that *both* parties benefited from the venture. So both sides had relationship managers who worked out any difficulties that arose and thereby ensured that the relationship blossomed into longer-term contracts.

In this way, ITNet saved its $2 million contract, and Esso UK saved hundreds of thousands of dollars in supplier changeover costs. After examining several hundred IT outsourcing projects, Kern and Willcocks concluded that formalizing the relationship-management role is a best practice.[17] In an outsourcing project, it is critical to empathize with and understand—on an ongoing basis—where the other firm is.

The most important of Willcocks and Kern's conclusions is that it's not simply nice to have such firm-to-firm relationships in outsourcing. It's that such relationships are *required* to mitigate the risk of both companies. These relationships are *not* touchy-feely; as we have said before, they are critical to the financial success of the project.

POINTS TO REMEMBER

Overview

>> Empathy creates healthy business and social relationships in which we feel connected, understood, and valued because we know that there is someone else who can imagine what it feels like to be us. Benefits of being able to empathize in business relationships:
  ○ Being able to adapt your problem-solving approach to get the best results for everyone.
  ○ People will like working with you and reciprocate by being empathetic toward you as well.
  ○ Save time and resources by being able to anticipate potential problems ahead of time.
  ○ There will be an increase in your ability to influence others without authority, that is, increase personal power.
  ○ It will lead to higher productivity and higher profitability.

>> The key to developing and growing strong business relationships lies in practicing empathy daily. For example, identifying the needs and expectations of others—be it people, other teams, or businesses—helps to
  ○ Look for a common ground.
  ○ Demonstrate interest, respect, and appreciation for the other culture's traditions and way of life.
  ○ Cultivate openness and selflessness.

 ## For Individuals

>> Quite simply, people long to be valued. Being empathetic shifts the focus away from you and allows others to be heard. By walking in their shoes, you help them to fulfill that need while at the same time gaining valuable insight into their world.

>> Most people will land somewhere between the extremes of Rob Bennett (highly empathetic) and Jason (our friend with Asperger's syndrome).
- At which end of the spectrum do you fall?
- What can you do to actively become more adept at walking in another's shoes?

 For Teams

>> When team members are unable—or unwilling—to walk in the shoes of their coworkers, it is easy for situations such as Gloria's to take place.
- Has a team member ever failed to ask you for your input? Would your information have helped to shape the outcome?
- Have you ever forgotten to practice empathy when making a decision that affected multiple members of your team? Do you think that there might have been unintended consequences for your actions?
- Think of a time where someone was empathetic to you and how that positively affected the quality of that relationship.

>> Practicing empathy should take place outside your team as well. Placing yourself in the shoes of other teams within your organization can prevent the *silo effect*, help to identify ways of working together better, and streamline processes—ultimately reducing stress and unnecessary work.

 For Organizations

>> In this global world with its interconnected cultures, firms, and supply chains, we have to be adaptable, bridge our differences, and adjust our working styles to work harmoniously with people and businesses who think differently, who see the world differently, and who have different habits.

>> Listening to our customers proves our commitment to service while at the same time allows us to see our product through their eyes. Operation Bear Hug revealed insights

and product opportunities to IBM's top executives that would have otherwise gone undiscovered.

» Done genuinely, empathy can deeply strengthen the relationship between brand and consumer as well. When Southwest Airlines asked its passengers to put themselves in the shoes of the flight attendant whose family member was in a car accident, it was able to explain the situation while creating an emotional bond.

NOTES

_____
_____
_____
_____
_____
_____
_____
_____
_____
_____
_____
_____
_____
_____
_____
_____
_____

Whether People Trust You Is Often up to You

Mutual trust is part of the DNA of any effective business relationship. It is unspoken and based on what one friend called truth over time. As Bruce Barnes, former CIO, says, "In my football days, there were people I played next to whom I never had to look at to know exactly where they were and what they were doing. I just knew because we'd done enough together that I knew what they were thinking and how they were responding to given situations. As a result, collectively, we could anticipate with confidence and purpose. The same is true in an effective business relationship."[1]

We have already seen that individuals, teams, and companies can get better results when there are strong business relationships. So why is trust so important, how does trust work, what characteristics of trust most affect relationships, and how can you get business associates to trust you more? We'll look at the practices that some skillful relationship developers use to increase trust and what you might do to develop these same practices.

Why Is Trust So Important?

Trust is the foundation of all powerful social and business relationships. As we mentioned earlier, at the heart of any business relationship is the notion of reciprocity. That is, I will help you, and in return, I expect that you will help me.[2] Therefore, trust is critical to healthy relationships between individuals, within teams, and throughout organizations. Trust allows us to feel safe and to take risks. It allows us to be ourselves.

What Does Trust Look Like?

In the social exchange theory, relationships are built on reciprocity. Unless we're being philanthropic (and even sometimes then), when we help someone, we often assume that they will help us back at some point. When the reciprocity is even or balanced, we have established a level of trust. When we believe we're giving more than we're receiving, we may decide that we cannot trust that person as we had hoped. Perhaps he or she is not as committed to the relationship as we are. Either way, trust is diminished.

Trust speeds things up because it reduces the need for people—or businesses—to consistently prove their value. Shared trust allows all parties to feel safe and empowered to do their best. Trust reduces the number of miscommunications and friction. Generally, problem solving is easier when trust (e.g., sincerity, reliability, and competence) has been proven. As a result, trusting relationships are stronger and more powerful, generally requiring less "upkeep." Again, they allow us to work together more efficiently and effectively.

So how do I know a high-trust relationship when I see one? Think of a business colleague. How many of the following things describe your relationship?

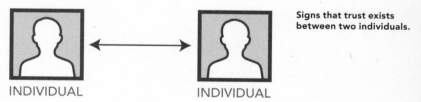

INDIVIDUAL   INDIVIDUAL

Signs that trust exists between two individuals.

>> The relationship is reciprocal. There is usually equal give and take.
>> There is a balance of power.
>> You know that you can count on each other. You know that the person has your back.
>> You want the best for each other.
>> You can say what you mean without a filter and be accepted—and respected—for who you are, not whom they would like you to be. In other words, you don't have to pretend to be something you're not. In fact, they won't let you get away with pretending.
>> You know you're safe with this person.

What Is Trust?

Trust is one of those words that can mean many different things to different people. When you say that you trust or don't trust someone, what do you mean?

Although there have been seemingly countless academic articles attempting to more clearly define trust, we have found it most helpful to think of trusting business relationships resting on three pillars:

1. *Sincere intent.* Do I believe that you truly care about my well-being? Are you really well intended toward me?
2. *Reliability.* Can I count on you to keep your promises?
3. *Competence.* Do I believe that you are competent to do this particular task?[3]

Let's explore this by starting with *sincere intent.* If we question someone's sincerity, we are questioning his or her intent. Does the person wish me good or ill? Can I count on the person to tell me the

Pillars of Trust

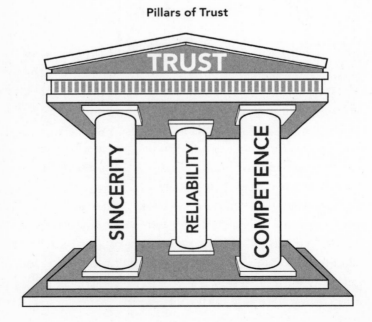

truth? Am I safe with this person, or will he or she stab me in the back?

We have to be careful here because it is easy to jump to a conclusion or misdiagnose the situation. For example, if someone tells you that a fellow employee criticized you behind your back to your boss, it is easy enough to check that out either by asking the person directly in a fact-checking or nonthreatening kind of way or by simply asking your boss. Too often, eyewitness testimony is unreliable, so you always need to make certain that comments were heard accurately or that something was not taken out of context. If it turns out, however, that your colleague was indeed spreading falsehoods about you, you may find it difficult to recover the relationship with him.

For most of us, then, when someone says, "I'm not sure I trust him," people usually assume that we are questioning his sincerity or intent. For example, we once worked on another company's project team with Frances (not her real name). She was reliable in that she met deadlines and did what she said she would, but numerous people had suggested that she was passively sabotaging the project. In other words, they questioned her sincerity. To sort this out, her boss met with her and our team to see if we could uncover the problem. During the meeting, though, Frances sarcastically admitted that she honestly did not care if the people or the project succeeded. She was sick of the whole thing! In fact, she said that she had secretly hoped that the project would soon fail so that she could take a vacation. At that point, the discussion was over. There was no trusting her. Had she been unreliable, the boss could have instituted follow-up processes; had she been incompetent, he could have provided training; in the case of insincerity, there was nothing more he could do. Everyone had now lost trust that she would work productively for the project's successful completion. The team could not risk it; her boss removed her from the project and the company. He could not fix her malign intent.

We maintain that whether or not someone trusts you is often up to you. This is the case with sincerity. You can generate this level of trust (sincerity) if you are clear about your intent upfront. For example, saying, "The reason I need you to share that information with me is . . ." or "My intent in asking these questions is to . . ." allows people an insight into your intent. It helps them know where you are coming from.

Sometimes, though, you may find the need to double check your intent. Sometimes we say that we want to help, but underneath we may instead want to prove a point. It's tricky. We find this particularly true when giving feedback. Are you trying to really get a dig in or are you actually trying to help by providing objective data? When you use sarcasm, are you *really* kidding? Sometimes it's hard to know. As Jose Acevedo, a colleague and an expert in developing high-performing teams says, "We don't wear psychic Pampers." This means our ill-intent can leak into the relationship, whether or not we express it. Like it or not, people can often feel our intent. So getting clear about your intent before you speak is important.

Sincerity is a key pillar on which trust rests. But by itself, it isn't enough. You may be honest and sincerely care about someone and their business, yet they may not fully trust you. This brings us to the other two pillars: reliability and competence.

Reliability can be defined as keeping your word, your promises. In other words, do you do what you say you will do? For example, if you promise that you will call me back in five minutes, do you? If you say that you will copy me on all future correspondence, do you? If you say that you will have the draft report to me by Friday noon, is it there by noon? In other words, do I trust that I can count on you?

Reliability may be the most important aspect of trust. As Angelo Mazzocco, president of the Pillar Technology Group, an innovative business and technology consulting firm, told us:

Do what you say you're going to do. If you set an expectation with people, then deliver on your expectation. Reputation is everything. It tells you something about a person when he or she doesn't deliver. I always take notes on what I need to follow up on. I also always try to find a way to help people. How can I do a favor for them? You can't expect to do something for everyone, but if I commit to doing something for someone, I always make sure to follow through.[4]

Lack of reliability is easy to spot if goals are clearly aligned and expectations clearly defined. The problems come when we say that someone is unreliable, but there were unclear expectations (what if he does not know, for example, what you want him to do specifically, by when, and in what format?). What if there was a lack of clarity as to whether there actually was an agreement or just an assumption? For example, did you request that you receive the file by 4 o'clock? Did that person say, "Yes, I will send you the file by 4 o'clock." Or did you simply assume that the person would do so? Were you clear? Did the person understand?

If expectations were clear, though, and there was clear agreement to completing the task, then it is fair to assume that that person is unreliable if he does not keep his promises. If that is the case, then our trust in him starts to suffer.

In many of our interviews, executives and managers made the importance of promises clear. A president of a very successful company in Texas who asked to remain anonymous commented:

When you do make a commitment, stick to it. That's how you build trust with people. They realize your handshake, your word, is your bond. Sounds old-fashioned, but that's what it is. If you shake a guy's hand and agree to something, you've agreed to it. You don't need a document. Now the document may be necessary because that's what we need these days. But with or without documents, be sincere about what you are saying and what you are agreeing to. Only agree to something if you intend to do it.

There is a solid story about how Coca-Cola won consumers' trust in Europe after a bad episode. In early June 1999, more than 240 people in Belgium and France reported intestinal problems after drinking Coke. The Belgian government banned Coke products for 10 days. Even though there was no clear evidence that Coke's products were causing these health problems, Coke decided to recall beverages from five European countries, 17 million cases in total, making it the biggest recall in Coke's history.

CEO Douglas Ivester publicly stated: "For 113 years our success has been based on the trust that consumers have in that quality. That trust is sacred to us."

Rather than waiting on legally defending itself, Coke's executives apologized and assumed responsibility for whatever happened. They also identified two quality-control problems that may have potentially led to this situation. During this crisis, Coke offered to cover health-care costs for all those affected. It also offered free products to every single one of the 4.4 million homes in Belgium. Though later it was found that the reported health problems were not caused by Coke, Coke's act of empathy went a long way not just in rebuilding consumer trust but also in increasing it significantly. Three years after the scandal, sales in Belgium were reportedly better than ever. As stated in a *Sloan Management Review* article, Coke thanked its customers more than ever for their loyalty, and by the beginning of August (fewer than 2 months after the incident), research indicated that core consumers of Coca-Cola products reported the same levels of intent to purchase as before the crisis had hit.[5]

This story shows that in times of crisis, what differentiates high-integrity firms is the degree to which they quickly accept responsibility and show genuine concern for their customers. As you can see, empathy restored trust and won the day for Coke.

Like it or not, relationships—particularly business relationships—are not static. They ebb and flow depending on

>> The amount of turnover in the contact person(s) with whom you're dealing
>> Leadership's changing priorities

>> Changing market demands
>> Technology innovations
>> Cultural shifts

Powerful people work hard at making clear requests and promises. They make certain that they understand what is being asked of them, and they are willing to say "No" if they believe that they cannot do what was requested. Over time, these leaders learn to commit only to the things they are able to accomplish. They understand that "I'll try" is not a commitment to completing the request. Furthermore, if they suddenly realize that they have to revise or revoke their promise, they let people know immediately. They understand that although someone will be disappointed, by communicating bad news early, the other party will have more time to react.

This is a foundation for building reliability. By defining the expectations of the buyer and then executing those deliverables within the time frame promised, the relationship's trust level grows over time.

Each part of the business struggles with this issue of reliability in its own way:

Salespeople wonder if they have to overpromise to make the sale or should say that the order will take longer than expected. Customer-service reps wonder what to do if they know that a problem is a chronic customer complaint, but they are instructed by their employer not to reveal that. Operations people know that there is a higher degree of process failure in one particular area of the business, but they have to make commitments anyway. Research and development departments believe that the product will work in most situations but have to certify that it will work in all situations. And on it goes. Whatever part of the company you are in, it is important that you look at the promises you—and your team or department—make and find some way to track them to help ensure greater reliability and, thus, trust.

Finally, there is the trust related to *competence*. That is, do I trust your ability to do a specific task, diagnosis a problem, or make an informed decision? We can trust a person's intent and reliability but not trust their expertise or skill set. Let's look at an example.

Recently, an aunt of one of the authors was in the hospital recovering from hip surgery resulting from a bad fall. In the process of recovering from the surgery, she developed large sores on the left side of her face. The surgeon insisted that these were due to the fall. Although we trusted the surgeon's commitment to our aunt's well-being, and we knew that we could count on him to give us expert orthopedic advice, we did not trust that he was competent to diagnose skin diseases. Only when the family called in a skin specialist did we learn that she had developed shingles and that there needed to be significant changes in her care and treatment plan.

In business, we face these types of trust situations all the time. We may trust a person's intent and reliability but perhaps not his competence in a particular area. If competence is the issue, additional training might lead to higher trust. If reliability is a problem, it might help to lay out the performance requirements for jobs, thus laying out guidelines for success. If we have ample evidence that the person does not sincerely care about us, trust is tough, if not impossible, to restore. In such a case, the best we can do is to extricate ourselves from the relationship. If that's not possible, then we need to understand that, like it or not, we will always be in a win-lose negotiation in any situation with that person.

Most of us are lucky to be on even one high-performing team in our lives, let alone in our business careers. These teams are so rare and so powerful that our other team experiences might be frustrating and/or disappointing.

To look at team trust more closely, look at a story about the 2011 Nebraska women's volleyball team, rated second in the country. Lauren Cook, the team's number one setter (the person who places the ball so that another team member can spike it) was arrested for leaving the scene of an accident involving an injury and could not play for two games. During those games, did the team then fall apart? No—it simply refocused on the trust that the players had in themselves and their coach (who is also Lauren's father). John Cook took time off from coaching to spend more time with Lauren.

In 2011, without its No. 1 setter, Nebraska's No. 2–ranked volley-ball team re-learned the meaning of the most important word in the Huskers' vocabulary: T-R-U-S-T. John Cook and Lauren Cook couldn't have been prouder about the way Dan Conners [the assistant coach] took on some of the head coach's responsibilities and the way senior captain Brigette Root [the backup setter] stepped in for Lauren and kept Nebraska's season in lockstep progress while Lauren Cook dealt with the most difficult time in her life. Ten years ago, John Cook made this observation: "Trust. Without it, there's no team. Of the teams I've coached that have been success-ful, all have had an unbelievable amount of trust in each other."

In his first year as a Nebraska assistant, Conners has seen a high-character team reinforce its inherent trust in each other. "It's a testament to Coach Cook and the way he runs the pro-gram," Conners told me. "It's also a testament to his players on how they've learned to respond to a difficult situation. Trust has been the theme for this team—from the big changes in new play-ers and the new staff to participating in a news conference. We knew trust was going to be a big issue this year, and that's been the point of emphasis for our players and staff all year. We've all taken it to heart and learned how to trust in ourselves and each other. It's something Coach Cook believes, I believe, the team believes, and the staff believes. We all know you can go a lot far-ther collectively than you can on your own, and we all know that it takes a lot of trust to do that."

Brigette Root exemplifies Nebraska volleyball trust like no one else. Cook calls Root, his backup setter, "Rudy" because as a walk-on, she embodies the team-first spirit. She not only sets the standard for work ethic, but also earns the respect of her team-mates. Cook says Root's probably earned more respect than any single player he's ever coached. With that in mind, I couldn't help but ask Root, who graduated first in her high school senior class of 443, how important trust is in a grueling sport. "It's huge and what makes this team so successful," she said. "It's not something that's developed in a day or a week or a month. It's something we've been working on since last January and really hounded on when the freshmen came in. This team's been through a lot of adversity, and we've really stuck together through tough times. Our trust has grown even more and must continue to grow. We have a mission every day we go to practice. We know we're not the most talented team out there. We're not the biggest, the fastest, or the most physical, so we have to make up for that to be a great team. We have to trust each other."[6]

Nebraska, in its first season in the Big Ten, placed first in the conference.

Although in sports it is often easiest to see a team in action, we also see high-performing teams in many other areas. Watch the movie *Apollo 13* if you want to see another high-performing team in action. Basically, the story is this: *Apollo 13*, America's seventh manned space mission, was launched on April 11, 1970, with newly configured crew leadership. Two days later, an oxygen tank exploded approximately 200,000 miles above Earth, severely crippling the command module and requiring the crew to abort the lunar landing. Despite almost insurmountable odds aboard the command module, the crew was returned safely to Earth on April 17. Their safe return was seen as a modern miracle. But part of that miracle resulted from having built such a high-performing team that melded astronauts in the command module flying 200,000 miles above Earth and technicians on the ground in Mission Control. Aboard the command module, with limited power, lighting, food, and oxygen, and on the ground, every part of trust got tested within and between the two parts of the mission team: the sincerity of their intent, their reliability, and their competence. It forced them to collaborate, take calculated risks, and create innovative solutions that saved the day. That was a high-performing team in action.

A High-Trust Business

Renfro Foods, a gourmet food company specializing in hot and spicy foods, located in Forth Worth, Texas, operates primarily without contracts, and the company does million-dollar deals with customers. As Doug Renfro, the CEO, told us:

> We don't have contracts for the most part. Kroger can kick us out tomorrow—no warning. A distributor could kick us out tomorrow. We can fire our broker with 30 days notice; they can fire us with 30 days notice. It's a very handshake-oriented industry.... I think part of the need for having this trust and these relationships is that there is no paper to fall back on. A seven-figure customer can be a zero customer with no notice if they want.[7]

No paper to fall back on? Few businesses would even consider a huge deal without paper; their legal teams wouldn't let them, even if they wanted to. But if what you depend on is a handshake deal, you'd better be ready to make good on your word; if you don't, you won't last long in the business. Imagine how having no paper to fall back on might affect your firm's emphasis on relationships and trust. The "soft" relationship stuff would get "hard" in a hurry.

Developing Trust with Customers

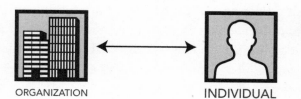

ORGANIZATION ← → INDIVIDUAL

Powerful relationships with customers require building trust over time.

You develop trust with customers—*both on a personal and a corporate level*—by being sincere, reliable, and competent *over time*. In the world of retail, Nordstrom's has been long known for trusting its customers so much that it will take back shoes, hats, shirts, and purses long after they were bought with no questions asked.

In the food business, Domonic Biggi, vice president of Beaverton Foods, the largest producer of nonrefrigerated horseradish and specialty mustards in the United States, tells the story of how his company has thrived as a result of trusting relationships:

> At the very beginning of our company, there was a guy who sold garlic on credit to my grandma when nobody else would. The same thing was true for a glass guy here in town. He, too, let her pay him off over time. After our business had been around for a while, we knew we could go get a better deal on garlic or glass, but because those people were there for us in the early days and helped grandma or my dad out, we allowed them to make a little bit of a premium for a while.
>
> Eventually, though, we said, "We've been doing business together for a long time. You helped us in the old days, and we have been paying you a premium for a period of time. Now we want to make it right. We need to be more competitive, and we're giving you first option to bid for our business."[8]

Jeff Schwantz, 15+ year business-to-business relationship manager, develops relationships with customers by sincerely caring about their welfare and offering them a total solution. As he says:

> We talk a lot about delivering our whole firm. If you are bringing the right subject matter experts to the customer's table, checking your ego at the door, and continually asking, "What's the right thing to do for this customer?" we have found [that] we can be tremendously successful.
>
> We have an example right now where a few years ago we might have created a business-line [channel] conflict. One of my partners manages the relationship with one of my best customers today. When we looked carefully at the customer relationship, we saw that there was a better solution for this customer within my business line—a solution that better positions the customer and

their firm. When we proposed the solution, the customer said, "Wow, you guys really worked together for us." They were really impressed that we have their interests and strategic direction in mind and are putting those first. While in the past our focus was primarily product-based, we're now truly unlocking the value that would previously have been a single product sale. We found that when we didn't bring the right subject matter experts to the meeting, both we and the customer suffered.[9]

Only those who have gone through channel conflict and internal squabbling understand how difficult these steps are to perform, but those people know for sure that these steps must be done if they are going to sell their firm's competencies. So what's the payoff for completing these steps? Let Schwantz continue:

Our approach is more holistic than the piecemeal products; focus on providing solutions not products is a win-win for everybody. When you look at it from the standpoint of overall revenue, it's a no-brainer as we grow the relationship by developing the best overall solution for the customer.[10]

When we asked Schwantz what he thought were the biggest mistakes firms made when they tried to establish a trusting relationship with another firm, he said:

1. Not being direct! People so often try to sugar-coat bad news. That just does nobody any good.
2. Only having a relationship with the top person—whoever makes decisions—and no one else at the customer. That's a house of cards in my mind. I think it's better to be approachable at any level of an organization, and it's important that we recognize the supporting organization as well.
3. People wanting to take shortcuts and pretend to be experienced in their industry—they "try to fake it till they make it." I am old school—you just better know your stuff.

4. People not admitting a screw-up soon enough. You've got to admit it, and then do something to restore their trust.[11]

Schwantz told us that *trust is much more than a nice thing to have. He said that trust is a bottom-line requirement for maximizing a firm's profitability.* Schwantz hopes that his competitors keep seeing relationship building as a soft issue because his firm is differentiating itself by developing into a trusted advisor for his customers. *And it's paying off in hard dollars.*

Trust Speeds Things Up

Stephen M. R. Covey, in his *The Speed of Trust*, argues that greater trust speeds transactions, lowers costs, and raises profits:

Warren Buffett, CEO of Berkshire Hathaway and one of the most trusted business leaders in the world, does million-dollar agreements on mere handshakes and lets the legal people work out the contract. Let's look at how such high levels of trust won the day for both Berkshire Hathaway and Wal-Mart during Berkshire's acquisition of McLane Distribution from Wal-Mart. Usually, mergers of this scale and between such big companies cost several million dollars to pay for the accountants, auditors, lawyers, etc. and take many months to complete. However, in this merger, things were different, as in just one two-hour meeting (in place of six months or more) and a handshake, the merger took just a month to complete. Speaking about this merger, Mr. Buffett added, "We did no 'due diligence.' We knew everything would be exactly as Wal-Mart said it would be—and it was." From saving the due diligence costs to cutting down on the six months or more time frame, the high-trust worked financial wonders for both parties.[12]

Only those who have gone through a complex merger know how much time and money had been saved.

Jim Hallett, CEO of KAR Auction Services, amplifies that conclusion when he says:

> A guy once told me most things in life can be taken away from you except your integrity; you've got to give that away. And that is true. The most important thing is when people look at you, do they see you as genuine, as sincere, do they believe you, do people have confidence in what you are saying, and do people trust you? At the end of the day, life is really about people trusting you. And when people trust you, you accelerate everything you do with that person or firm.[13]

Bruce Barnes, former Fortune 100 CIO and current faculty member at The Ohio State University, makes the same point in a slightly different way, saying:

> Gaining trust is not unlike the centrifugal force experienced when spinning a rock on a string. As you start shortening the string, the rock turns faster and more productively; however, in doing so, the force that could potentially throw your back out increases as well. As you go closer toward the axis, the more work is needed to get there ... and the faster you will be expelled if that trust is broken. In today's multiple-moving-parts world, no one has the luxury of floating down a lazy river to the center of trust, power, and influence. We are in a time-compressed environment with high demands for performance, and we cannot do that alone. Our levels of success (or not) will be directly proportionate to the levels of effective, productive, trusted relationships we have built along the way.[14]

What to Do When Establishing Trust Is Impossible

Let's keep it real-world here. What if suppliers start off by not having your firm's best interests at heart? We had a friend (let's call him Ed) who worked for a global engineering firm. The firm had a huge two-year project in Great Britain that was not doing well after three months, and Ed was asked to go in and turn the project around.

Ed was and is a gifted relationship manager. One of his subordinates said about Ed's people skills that he had "antennae on his antennae." He had been warned about the British subcontractors on the project, who in some cases had made more from the lawsuits on a botched project than they did on the original work. But he did not want to go in biased, so he met with the subcontractors and could tell very quickly that he could not depend on support from them. The suppliers had buffaloed his firm's previous project manager, and Ed saw clearly and quickly that they were going to try to buffalo him as well.

What do you do when the trust is simply not there? Where does one start? Delicately stated, if your firm has committed to the project, you do the project, and you cover your backside. What Ed did immediately was to set up a database that monitored project performance as well as what happened every day on the project—what was requested of the suppliers, what was produced, and an explanation of any disagreements. To be successful, the project had to maintain a certain level of performance over a certain number of months, and Ed made sure that he hit—and recorded—the performance targets. At the end of the project, though, as Ed had expected, the subcontractors banded together and sued Ed's firm for what they claimed were contractual lapses.

Then came the trial. Because the project was very technical, and because Ed was gifted in downshifting his technical vocabulary, he became the only person in the courtroom who could explain to the judge and jury the technical terms, requirements, and performance issues. So—even though he was the one being sued—he became the critical expert witness in the courtroom. Whenever things got confusing—and some of the issues were very confusing—the judge or the defense attorney and sometimes even the prosecuting attorney would turn to Ed for a translation. And as he helped the judge and jury, he quickly established relationships with them. The prosecuting attorneys hated it, but the judge and jury were very grateful to have someone to explain what it was all about. But Ed had more than his people skills. Ed was the only person who had a project diary detailing every day he had been on the job. Those suing never thought of such a record. They assumed it would be their word against Ed's. But Ed was able to show—almost hour by hour—what had gone on, who performed effectively, and who had not. He also had the printouts showing that the project had indeed delivered what the contract specified.

Ed's firm, having lost other British multi-million-dollar lawsuits in the past, initially was concerned that it would have to pay out tens of millions of dollars. But Ed's database demolished the sub-contractors' story. The firm was so grateful that it gave Ed a huge bonus and from that point on required that its project managers maintain a detailed project diary. Gifted relationship managers can usually tell who is on their side. Ed followed the dictates of his antennae, a wise move, and ended up living the advice of Finley Peter Dunne, a great twentieth-century American humorist, who once said, "Trust everybody—but cut the cards."

Why Is Achieving Trust in Business So Hard?

It's difficult to trust another business because what it takes to be trustworthy as an organization is demanding, difficult, and complex. In the early 1980s, Valarie Zeithaml, Leonard Berry, and A. Parasuraman published a series of articles that defined service-quality expectations from a customer's point of view. The articles were then turned into what we think is a business classic, *Delivering Quality Service: Balancing Customer Perceptions and Expectations*. In the book, the three authors provide the five determinants of service quality, which are listed below in descending level of importance:

1. *Reliability.* Ability to perform the promised service dependably and accurately
2. *Responsiveness.* Willingness to help customers and provide prompt service

3. *Assurance.* Knowledge and courtesy of employees and their ability to convey trust and confidence
4. *Empathy.* Caring, individualized attention the firm provides its customer
5. *Tangibles.* Appearance of physical facilities, equipment, personnel, and communication materials[15]

Their definition of service quality relates directly to trust *because it points out what a seller has to do to be perceived as trustworthy.* When most people think about service quality, they tend to think of customer service, and when they think about customer service, they tend to think about the importance of hiring employees with empathy. Although that is important, it is necessary but not sufficient. In fact, empathy is fourth in importance on Zeithaml's list. Our other perceptions of reliability, responsiveness, and assurance, in one way or another, all have a greater impact on the level of trust. Without these, perceived service quality, as well as trust, is low.

As we see it, service quality is a detailed performance issue. To be consistently reliable and responsive over time, you have to have set up systems that allow you to be reliable and responsive. You also have to have excellent customer listening and feedback systems as part of the process.

As Domonic Biggi, vice president of Beaverton Foods, says about firms that have screwed up and tried to fix the problem with some small gift: "In this day and age, it's just easy to send a bottle of wine and an 'I'm sorry' note or something, a token, instead of actually doing what's required to make it right."[16]

A gift won't right the relationship—you have to create a system to prevent the problem from ever happening again. Taking responsibility for problems and then taking immediate steps to keep them from happening again not only fixes the problem but usually dramatically increases the level of trust.

We would assert, therefore, as W. Edwards Deming did in a different context, that delivering reliability is only possible through some carefully designed system or process.

Assurance is a related but slightly different issue. If you have ever worked with a large firm, you may have noticed that smooth executives often sell you the project, and then, when the job is to be done, the people who do the work are younger and far less experienced. That hands-off is how many of these large firms make their money—it's their business model. Hire lots of young, smart people to support a much smaller number of seasoned professionals.

Other firms differentiate themselves by emphasizing the expertise of the most senior professionals—the person who sells the project is the person who manages the relationship, guides the work, and provides the assurance that the client will get a top-quality result. In other words, you can often trust these firms more because the people with whom you work not only care about you, but over time they have also seen what works and what does not. They are the most competent, and they are the ones who are working directly with you to solve your problems.

To be responsive, a firm must feel the need to deliver on promises made, and it must give front-line people the ability to move heaven and earth if it looks as if a promise is not going to be made. As Biggi says:

> If people don't trust you, they are not going to do business with you. It comes back to we told them we would sell the product at this price and give it to them on that day. If we don't, they don't trust us. They have options. These days you get companies that buy and sell everything. But if you get a new wave of people in there, policies and procedures and systems all change—it can give the customers whiplash. I'm lucky that we've had the same ownership here since 1985 and beyond that my grandma. We haven't had any significant changes; we've been very consistent. Customers know they are going to get what they ordered on time. That builds trust.[17]

Assurance also includes "knowledge and courtesy of employees." These are a matter of careful selection and training. Whoever that employee is, from a driver to a courier to an executive, when that person interacts with a customer, he or she *is* the company. If he or she doesn't know the answer to a customer question and guesses, he or she can end up making an impossible commitment. So, among other things, employees have to be trained to know the business inside and out. They have to learn that saying, "I don't know, but I can find out in 24 hours and get back to you" is a much better response than guessing. "The ability to convey trust and confidence" goes back to knowing themselves, their company, and their industry.

Assurance also is a matter of explaining things to the customer in a way the customer can understand. For example, every firm culture in our experience creates acronyms as internal communication shortcuts. If the company buries a customer with this internal language that the customer does not understand, it does not foster confidence or trust. In fact, it may raise more questions and a lack of certainty that the customer will be getting what she needs.

Empathy, as we discussed earlier in Key #2, tells people that you care about them and that you are willing to understand what it is like to walk in their shoes. For some people, it's nearly impossible to train empathy. Nurses by nature are expected to be empathetic and caring. If they are technically competent, but not empathetic, they do not usually achieve high degrees of professional success. Engineers, on the other hand, are not expected to be particularly empathetic, but when they are empathetic, as well as sincere, reliable, and competent, they can be wildly successful. They develop powerful business relationships and usually achieve amazing results and significant professional rewards. We saw this earlier with Bill Lantz.

Tangibles often have an indirect impact on whether or not you are caring, sincere, reliable, and competent. When visiting a doctor or dentist for the first time, you have no way to judge their performance. Thus we tend to make an evaluation based on things we can see, such as the office waiting area, examination room, and degrees on the wall. This is what Zeithaml calls "intangibles," and it helps us to evaluate providers we haven't dealt with before.

In summary, Zeithaml's first four determinants of service quality form the basis for trust in the customer's—or supplier's—mind. Did the customer get what he ordered on time? Did you respond quickly and effectively to a customer issue? Were you careful to be courteous and downshift your technical vocabulary with the customer? Did you identify with the customer's needs? A positive answer to these questions requires not just a one-word response but the design and delivery of systems and processes to make sure that all these things happen. Relationships are perhaps more difficult to maintain than they are to develop because developing trust in these areas cannot be left to chance.

POINTS TO REMEMBER

Overview

>> Trust is the foundation of all powerful social and business relationships. Trusting business relationships are built on three pillars:
- Sincerity
- Reliability
- Competence

>> Trust in business relationships is important because it
- Allows all parties involved to feel safe, empowered, capable, and able to do their best
- Reduces the number of miscommunications and friction between people
- Eases the problem solving, thereby speeding up the transactions
- Requires less upkeep in maintaining the business relationship

>> Finally, as a result, all the preceding lower costs and raise profits.

For Individuals

>> In high-trust business relationships, the connection is reciprocal. There is a balance of power, there is an assurance of having each other's back, there is a shared vision of wanting the best for each other, there is no pretense in words or actions, and there is a sense of safety and security in the relationship.

>> Think about the most trusted relationship you have with another colleague. What makes this relationship special? And how does that trust affect the way you communicate and work together?

For Teams

>> High-trust teams are capable of producing consistent, high-quality work because of the sincerity, reliability, and competence that exists among their members. Often the talents of one team member pick up where another's ended, creating a continuum of skill necessary to complete a project.

>> How much trust exists within your team? What is preventing that level from being higher?

>> Is there a high level of trust between departments in your organization? Which of the three pillars is missing (they may be different from department to department)?

 For Organizations

>> Achieving trust in business relationships, especially with customers, is hard because there are many demanding and complex service-quality expectations to be lived up to in order to gain that trust.

>> Five key determinants of these perceptions are: reliability, responsiveness, assurance, empathy, and tangibles.

>> Developing trust with customers is key to developing strong customer relationships over time. One key to developing these relationships is to be direct and not sugar-coat bad news, to be approachable through any level in the customer's organization, to know your stuff well, and to admit and accept responsibility for mistakes rather than hiding them.

>> There are certain relationships where trust just does not exist even if you did all that it takes. In such relationships, it is important to be worldly wise, cover your facts well, and be prepared for the worst.

>> Do your customers trust your organization? If not, which of the five key determinants do not exist?

NOTES

KEY #4

Share Information to Increase Your Personal Power

There is a proud and unfortunate history of people not sharing information—in all fields. Let's examine a historical case in which unshared information led to confusion on the battlefield. During the American Civil War, Robert E. Lee and Stonewall Jackson were considered the South's two greatest generals. But their leadership styles were wildly different.

Although both generals were audacious and strategic, Jackson was almost paranoid about plans leaking to the enemy, so he ended up not sharing—sometimes even with his direct-report generals—exactly what was required of them in battle. Lee, on the other hand, always had a prebattle meeting with his generals, in which he laid out the battle's objectives, asked for their input, and then set them loose to gain their objectives by the way they decided was best.

Lee's communication style worked very well—he won more battles than any other Civil War general—but Jackson's style hampered his effectiveness, at least in the first 12 months of the war. In a number of battles, Kernstown and Cedar Mountain among them, some of Jackson's generals were unsure what they were supposed to be doing, where they were supposed to be doing it, or even when the battle would begin. At Kernstown, for example, Jackson neglected to tell Brigadier General Richard Garnett—his second in command—exactly what his responsibilities were, and when Garnett did not achieve what Jackson expected, Jackson brought him up for court martial. Garnett represented himself. At one point Garnett asked Jackson exactly what the plan of battle had been for Kernstown. Jackson replied, "[T]o defeat the enemy by gaining heights on his right, which commanded his position, pressing on towards Winchester, then turning his right and getting in his rear." Garnett then asked, "Did you communicate this plan to me before or during the action?" Jackson said, "I did not to my recollection."[1] But Jackson refused to drop the charges. It took General Lee to straighten things out, but Garnett and Jackson continued to hate one another until Jackson died at Chancellorsville.

Garnett later described what it was like to have Jackson as a commander from December 1861 to April 1862, saying:

> Much of the greater portion of this time I was second in command. Yet General Jackson never conferred or advised with me in any important matter, except on a single occasion, when he called me to a council with the regimental commanders of my Brigade. I was thus kept in [as] profound ignorance of his plans, instructions and intentions as the humblest private in his army.[2]

Jackson apparently believed that if his generals were good soldiers, they would somehow divine what he required of them. This was not an effective approach for a leader, as some of his early battles bore out. If you have ever had a boss who refused to share information—for whatever reason—you know exactly how Garnett felt.

What Happens When Businesspeople Don't Share Information?

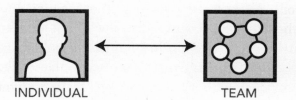

INDIVIDUAL   TEAM

Are you growing the relationship with your team by sharing necessary information? Or are you damaging it by withholding critical information?

So many organizations could thrive if their executives, managers, and employees would learn to share information, and we mean information in its broadest sense. Why don't they share? They may believe that their expertise is power—the school of "whoever knows the most wins." They may believe that if they share their knowledge, they won't get credit for solutions other people create (and they may well have had that happen). If somebody says, "Hey, could you help me with this?" and you give them everything you've got and then go to a meeting and they present your material as theirs, you may never share with that person again. However, if you give them everything you've got, and they go to a meeting and say, "Steve and I worked on this, and he really helped me," you get recognized for it, and you'll continue to share with that person. Bosses may also not share information because it never occurs to them that others may need the information or because sharing can be so time consuming.

We've also seen this lack of sharing many times with those who manage large business customers. Some don't want anybody else in the company even visiting the account. Others may not want to share their account profiles and plans because there may be a disparity between their plans and what the account manager has been telling the firm. In other cases, account managers withhold information because if nobody else knows about it, the company can't criticize the account manager.

Account information is a strategic asset for your firm—but only if it's shared. We have seen too many times what happens when it's not. The account manager, for one reason or another, can leave your firm and—because she knows more about that account than anyone—can either take that account with her or leave the account and the company stranded. And the lifetime revenue of that account disappears because the firm did not recognize the value of that hoarded information. This can be a very hard lesson for any business. On the other hand, if the organization recognizes the asset value of the information, it can provide processes and incentives for the account manager to share critical account data. Then, as the conduit of such information from large customers, the account manager can become invaluable to both the supplier and the customer.

We believe that the decision to share or withhold information can often be traced to a cultural issue. Do your firm's leaders share information? Do your executives acknowledge employees who share information? Do your executives promote collaboration? In our experience, if information sharing is not promoted from the top, it's not likely to be valued elsewhere in the business.

When Leaders Share Information

Tom Feeney, president and CEO of Safelite Group, Inc., parent company of Safelite AutoGlass, the largest provider of replacement auto glass in the United States, is one executive who has created a sharing culture. He told us: "I do think organizations take their cue from a leader. So, if you're creating an environment that respects relationships, encourages others to care about one another, then I think that starts to permeate from the leader down through their organization."[3] He first decided to focus on his employees' needs and then started measuring and sharing a number of key business indicators. Feeney discussed with us how sharing information can create a caring corporate culture. Feeney explained:

> One of our executives came up with a term, "people first." Companies can choose to put their associates, their customers, or their shareholders first. Unfortunately, most companies never really decide which one is first, and they are just never as successful as they could be. So we went through an exercise of values, making a conscious effort to decide who came first, and we said our associates come first. But our actions said our people might be second or third. So we challenge: is that really true? We said, "Yes it is. But now we've got to change our behavior to reinforce it because we want to send the right signals." In essence, we were saying that great leadership and a great culture were needed to bring People First to life.[4]

When we asked how he reinforced employees first, Feeney described one of his major approaches:

> First, we decided the cornerstones that would drive our culture: leadership, talent, caring, and focus. We went further to give all

of our associates a pledge. We just turned those things into more friendly words like "You have the right to expect great leadership. And when you don't get it, you have the responsibility to come forward."

Then we created an internal "Ask Tom" website for our associates. First, we tell them that the website is a safe environment, which means associates can ask any question they want and they'll get an answer in 72 hours. Now, I don't answer all of them directly. They go out to experts, but before an answer goes to the associate, I proof it, and I add my own little phrasing or change the wording, and I'm candid. If they tell us something that is not right, I fix it. I've been shocked at some of the things we've learned about this, but at the same time pleasantly surprised. And then we publish the question, the answer, and the fix on the website. We ask the person's permission to put the fix out there and whether it is okay to include their name. I'd say 98 percent say yes; 2 percent say no, they'd rather not. So then I go back and ask whether I could publish it anonymously. Everybody says yes to that. So we are at 2½ years into this part of our journey, and I'd say we are just starting to see the fruits of our labor.[5]

We asked Feeney to give us an example of an "Ask Tom" problem that he had solved, and he said:

I'll give you a good example here in this building [corporate head-quarters in Columbus, Ohio]. We had the handicapped spaces farther away, and a handicapped person wrote in and said it would be nicer if you had us right up to the front of the building. I went to the person in charge of that, and I said, "So why don't we do that?" Well, he gave me all sorts of reasons.... I said, so how bad would it be if we just changed it? He said, well, it wouldn't be bad at all. So change it. And we wrote back to the person and said by Monday you'll have new handicap spots. A pregnant woman wrote in ... and said she was having difficulty walking and she doesn't have a handicapped spot because, by our definition, she is not handicapped. When she comes to work at 10:00, the only spots left are really far away. So I went to the same person, and I said, so have you ever heard of an expectant mother spot? He said yeah, you see them at Babies 'R' Us or Toys 'R' Us. So let's make some. Today, if you go outside, there are four expectant mother spots.[6]

And how does this tie to developing a caring culture? Feeney continues, saying:

Honestly, I think associates' issues are usually easy to fix, and management, unfortunately, usually thinks it's too big to hear them out. I think you get great associate engagement when you do hear them out and you act on them, no matter how minor they seem. Because, to the employees, they are very significant or they wouldn't have written to you. I think that is all about building relationships. It's about showing employees you care. So, if caring is going to be for our people first, well you better damn well do something that shows you care.[7]

When we asked Feeney what results he'd seen over three years in creating a caring culture, he replied:

Higher engagement scores. Higher net promoter scores and how much better they are treating customers. Higher engagement leads to higher discretionary effort—a much better work product. It isn't about working harder ... working longer hours. It is just working smarter when you are here. Happier associates, I'd say.[8]

We need to clarify what Feeney is saying a bit. Higher engagement scores—how much employees feel they are a part of their company—can be measured, and Safelite does measure and share it. Higher net promoter scores—the percentage of customers who say they would recommend Safelite to others—is also measured. Currently, Safelite's net promoter score is 85 percent, which is world class. Feeney feels that there is a clear correlation between more engaged employees, higher net promoter scores, and financial results, and it's hard to argue with his results.

What are the financial results that are achieved by putting "people first" and correlating "employee engagement" and "net promoter scores"? Safelite's results can speak for themselves, although Feeney did not want to share the actual numbers. Over the last three years, both Safelite's revenues and margins are up by multiples. Safelite proves in spades Jim Heskett's thesis in *The Culture Cycle* that "as much as half the difference in operating profit between organizations can be attributed to an effective culture."[9]

There are other executives who work to develop a culture that makes it a value to share internal information. Jim Hallett, CEO of KAR Auction Services, Inc., has another way of hearing from his employees and sharing strategic and tactical information. He says that his executive assistant

> ... invites 20 people for breakfast from all departments. So we sit around and talk for an hour, hour and a half. We talk about personal stuff and about the company and its history, the vision for the company and where the company is going. And then at the end of that an electronic survey goes out with five very simple questions. It's unbelievable the impact that this meeting has on people. We talk a lot about culture and values in those meetings and how culture and values start and how we drive them and how we wrote them and how we got there. [10]

We noticed fairly early on in our executive interviews how many of our world-class relationship managers shared information by sending pertinent articles and books to their business friends and partners—both at their own firms and at others. As Tom Feeney says:

> I'm always routing articles around. And I think it stops that person for one minute, and they think of me and my company. People who believe in business relationships are always looking for some

unique way to allow the recipient to have that ten seconds of their time that creates a positive effect. Again, if I know someone really well and I know this particular topic of theirs that's important, and if I see a book, I'd buy them an extra copy and just shoot it in the mail to them. I don't overdo the social side of things. I don't overdo the golfing because I honestly think unless you've got a really special relationship, it makes most people uncomfortable. I keep it 85 percent business, 15 percent personal. But business is personal isn't it?[11]

Business *is* personal. And thriving in business requires both relationships and some way of recognizing and sustaining those relationships. Sharing information is a positive force if the information is truly relevant to the other person. One of the most helpful ways to work with a fellow employee is to ask: (1) what sort of information would be most relevant to him? (2) how would he like to get that information? (3) how often does the information need to be sent? and (4) would he please ask me the same questions? Without those types of questions, too much wrong information could easily be sent too often and in the wrong format. If you don't believe this, check your e-mail.

Derek Smith, former chairman and CEO of ChoicePoint, a data aggregation company, summarizes this idea by saying:

It is truly amazing when people realize that their opinion counts. The single greatest thing within a group is when each member of the group can say, "I know my opinion counts." Whether or not the opinion is accepted and whether or not it ultimately is chosen to be the path decided upon, the people feel like they were listened to, that they were heard and that they matter and it is then that the overall quality of the team goes up dramatically.[12]

3M shows what can happen if you just value people's opinions. Given today's communication technology, sharing information and getting insights by involving a large number of teams around the globe are great ways of uncovering breakthrough innovations. The senior vice president of strategy and corporate development challenged his planning group to come up with innovative ways to identify 3M's "markets of the future." In 2008, two gen Y analysts suggested using the "wisdom of the crowds" by engaging with and gathering ideas from thousands of 3M employees using technology. Making that happen was a huge task. The Information Technology (IT) Department selected a vendor to work with its team to house and create an online idea-sharing platform called *Innovation Live*. 3M's sales, marketing, and research and development (R&D) employees were invited to participate because they had strong customer relations and insights; the platform, however, was open to any 3M employee around the world who wanted to contribute. This live idea sharing went on for two weeks in April 2009. By the end of two weeks, 1,239 participants from 40 countries had generated 736 ideas, 6,799 quotes, and 1,084 comments. Innovation Live was a huge success because 3M was able to identify nine new markets as a result of this exercise. This also significantly increased employee engagement, and set the stage for many more such live idea-sharing programs.[13]

Sharing Proprietary Data to Thrive

One of the more interesting ways we have seen of creating dramatic growth is for a company to share its proprietary data, an approach that still remains unthinkable for most firms. Although many businesses define proprietary data as their primary strategic asset, there are cases where firms have shared such information and have improved their bottom lines substantially. The following two cases are taken from Don Tapscott and Anthony Williams' *Wikinomics: How Mass Collaboration Changes Everything*, which we highly recommend. Here is what happened with the Canadian gold-mining firm Goldcorp:

In 2000, Rob McEwen, CEO of Goldcorp, a Canadian gold-mining firm that was in trouble, did the unthinkable. He had his geologists put Goldcorp's geologic data—over 400 megabytes—on the Internet. He then initiated the "Goldcorp Challenge," offering $575,000 in prizes for entrants who could locate additional gold deposits. McEwen had gotten the idea of sharing proprietary data from Linus Torvalds, who had created the world-class computer operating system Linux. Torvalds had made public his operating codes and suddenly thousands of volunteer programmers were checking, improving, and adding to the operating system.

Goldcorp started receiving submissions from all over the world. McEwen had assumed that only geologists would reply, but he received suggestions from graduate students, consultants, mathematicians, and military officers. The entrants identified over 100 possible sites for gold, 50 percent of which had not been identified by Goldcorp. More important, over 80 percent of the targets yielded substantial quantities of gold. Since March 2000, through this contest, Goldcorp had found over 8 million ounces of gold on its 55,000 acres. McEwen said that the collaborative process had shaved two to three years off Goldcorp's normal exploration time.

In the end, although millions of ounces of gold were found, the true change from the challenge was that it transformed Goldcorp from an underperforming $100 million firm to a $9 billion juggernaut. One hundred dollars invested in Goldcorp in 1993 is worth $3,000 today.[14]

These new relationships developed with contestants led Goldcorp to great financial success. The other benefit, though, was Goldcorp learning from its contest winners wholly new ways to approach the problem of finding gold. As McEwen says, "Some of our contestants used applied math, advanced physics, intelligent systems, computer graphics, and [brought] organic solutions to inorganic problems.... When I saw the computer graphics, I almost fell out of my chair."[15] Sharing proprietary information provided wholly new ways to move the firm—and the industry—forward. Tapscott and Williams make the key point about this case of developing new working relationships. They say that McEwen

... realized the uniquely qualified minds to make discoveries were probably outside the boundaries of his organization, and by sharing some intellectual property, he could harness the power of collective genius and capability.... Welcome to the new world ... where collaboration on a mass scale is set to change every institution in society.[16]

The Lego blocks case from *Wikinomics* shows another way that the creativity of customers can be harnessed. If you have or had children, the odds are that you have these blocks in some part of your house—behind chairs and under bookcases—even if they have not been played with in years.

Although Lego still makes the interlocking plastic blocks, it has increasingly turned to more sophisticated products. In 1998, it introduced the Mindstorm series, where users can build real robots—and a great many other things—out of programmable bricks. Lego was astonished that Mindstorm was appealing not only to children but also to adult hobbyists. User groups began to spring up, and tinkerers had hacked into the programmable bricks, reprogramming the sensors, motors, and controller devices at the heart of Mindstorm.

When these user groups started submitting their creations, Lego initially threatened lawsuits. Users rebelled, and someone very smart at Lego finally saw the possibilities. From that point on, Lego allowed hacking, and thus set its users' imaginations loose. Today, the Lego website offers a free downloadable software development kit. In 2005, a Dutch Lego fanatic, using the development system, made a working pinball machine out of 20,000 Lego blocks. In effect, Lego allowed its users to become an integrated part of its design department. The company even allowed the most fanatical users to be a part of the team developing the 2005 Mindstorm upgrade, the NXT. Keep in mind that Lego does not pay its customers to offer these suggestions. While Lego will not say how much the design suggestions have added to its bottom line, the number must be substantial.[17]

We have no idea whether sharing proprietary data with the world could help you in your industry. We offer these cases as examples of shared data leading to massive and untapped creativity that dramatically raised two firms' bottom lines. If that impact can be harnessed in a hidebound industry such as mining or plastic blocks, are there possibilities for doing the same thing in your firm? Aside from purchasing your products, are there more ways that your customers could be helping you grow? Can you step outside the box, ask this question, and consider all sorts of answers? What sort of information might your customers need? This is a great topic for organizational brainstorming.

Sharing with Other Businesses

It is one thing to share proprietary data with people and customers. It is quite another to share such data with other businesses. And yet, in some cases, these information-based partnerships have led to major financial benefits to both firms. As one example, in the mid-1990s, such information sharing led to Toshiba computers being able to compete in the United States.

It took some time for United Parcel Service (UPS) to realize that one of its core competencies was logistics, but once it did, it led to one of the firm's most profitable spin-offs. In the early and mid-1990s, when Toshiba introduced its own laptop computers in the American market, the firm had no repair facilities in the United States. This meant that if there were any problems with a Toshiba PC, it had to be sent to Japan, and that meant that the user was without his PC for 8 to 10 days. No business user can be without his PC for that long, and as word about this began to spread, fewer and fewer businesspeople were purchasing Toshiba PCs.

UPS had the shipping contract from Toshiba, but when UPS saw that its delivery numbers were dropping, it analyzed the problem and came to Toshiba offering its logistics services. UPS would take over the repair of Toshiba laptops and thus drop substantially the turnaround time for repairs. Toshiba accepted the offer, even though it required sharing proprietary data with UPS employees. Toshiba trained UPS technicians to fix their PCs and set up a repair facility in Louisville, Kentucky. The turnaround time dropped from 8 to 10 days to under 4 days. Toshiba's sales went up, and suddenly UPS was shipping many more Toshiba products.[18] This is an excellent example of how two companies benefited by sharing information to deepen their relationships with each other.

Conclusion: For Want of a Word . . .

We have one last example in which the lack of sharing information and collaborating with others can lead to serious problems—even death. This occurred in a 1980's controlled study of flight crews under extreme stress situations conducted for the National Aeronautics and Space Administration (NASA). As James O'Toole and Warren Bennis described it:

> NASA researchers had placed existing cockpit crews—pilot, copilot, navigator—in flight simulators and tested them to see how they would respond during the crucial 30 to 45 seconds between the first sign of a potential accident and the moment it would occur. The stereotypical take-charge "flyboy" pilots, who acted immediately on their gut instincts, made the wrong decisions far more often than the more open, inclusive pilots who said to their crews, in effect, "We've got a problem. How do you read it?" before choosing a course of action. . . . But Blake and Mouton [the researchers] went deeper, demonstrating that the pilot's habitual style of interacting with their crews determined whether crew members would provide them with essential information during an in-air crisis. The pilots who'd made the right choices routinely had open exchanges with their crew members. The study also showed that the crew members who had regularly worked with the "decisive" pilots were unwilling to intervene— even when they had information that might save the plane.[19]

The study, we think, leads to some frightening implications for take-charge executives in a crisis situation who follow their own instincts without input from others. The need for openness and inclusion is not a nice-to-have. It's a *need-to-have*—if you want to thrive.

POINTS TO REMEMBER

Overview

>> Hoarding information (and having information hoarded from you) can create major crimps in your productivity and negatively affect relationships. When possible, track down the cause of those crimps, emphasize to those people that sharing is critical for the firm's thriving, and improve your firm's overall performance.

 ## For Individuals

>> Do you tend to keep information to yourself, share when needed, or overshare information with others? How does your preference affect the types of relationships you have with others, and what can you do to improve your style to increase the flow of information from both sides?

>> Think of a time when a friend or colleague shared a critical piece of information with you. How did it affect your relationship? How did it affect your situation?

 ## For Teams

>> Teams that share information are capable of achieving more output and greater impact with fewer people. That said, teams that share too much information run the risk of overwhelming members and slowing down processes.

>> Do you believe that sharing information empowers team members and enables everyone to accomplish more, or do you believe that hoarding information places you in a more powerful position?

>> How much information do you currently share with your team? Are you curating your efforts—sharing only the most critical pieces—or do you put everything out there, forcing team members to find the pieces that are important to them?

For Organizations

>> Creating a cooperative, sharing culture requires, among other things:

  ○ Creating strategic goals that provide clear goals for employees that can be tracked and reported

  ○ Making it safe to share constructive criticism—with every level of your organization

  ○ Developing systems by which to listen and respond to the needs of your employees

  ○ Reporting solutions so that all employees can see what has been done

>> Consider sharing appropriate firm data with others to create constructive ways to "harness the power of collective genius."

NOTES

_____

_____

_____

_____

_____

_____

_____

_____

_____

_____

_____

_____

_____

_____

Manage Yourself Before You Manage Others

Knowing yourself
is the beginning
of all wisdom.

—ARISTOTLE

There is growing emphasis on self-awareness a key characteristic of effective business people, especially leaders, in this world of networking and collaboration. That is because self-awareness allows us to be more aware of how we come across—and the more we understand that, the more effective we are likely to be.

What Is Self-Awareness?

If we are self-aware, we are clear—*we don't deceive ourselves*—about our strengths, limitations, hopes, emotional responses, *and* their impact on our behavior. In addition, we have a pretty good idea regarding how others see us and how we stack up against others. Coming to that clarity, though, is no easy task. As the Scottish poet Robert Burns says, "O wad some Power the giftie gie us to see oursels as ithers see us!"[1] To know ourselves deeply and clearly is hard work. Because self-awareness comes in part *through our reflection on feedback* from others, such feedback is indeed a gift. And this self-awareness can pay off big time. The extent to which we are self-aware—or not—can *profoundly* affect our professional and personal lives.

Daniel Goleman, in his seminal work on emotional intelligence, defines its two major components as *personal competence* and *social competence*. He defines *self-awareness*, an aspect of personal competence, as "knowing one's internal states, preferences, resources, and intuitions." Self-awareness includes

1. *Emotional awareness.* Recognizing one's emotions and their effects.
2. *Accurate self-assessment.* Knowing one's strengths and limits.
3. *Self-confidence.* A strong sense of one's self-worth and capabilities.[2]

To illustrate how interconnected decision making and feelings are, Goleman recounts the story of a "brilliant" corporate lawyer who, after having undergone successful surgery to remove a brain tumor, had lost his ability to make decisions, thus eventually losing everything that ever had been important to him—his job, family, and home. His life was in shambles. The lawyer sought help from Dr. Antonio Demasio, a neurosurgeon from the University of Iowa.

Dr. Demasio was able to explain the cause of the problem. During the surgery, "the surgeon accidently cut the circuits connecting the lawyer's prefrontal lobes with the amygdala." As a result:

> The lawyer had no *feeling*s about his thoughts and so no preferences. Demasio's conclusion was that our minds are not designed like a computer, to give us a neat printout of the rational arguments for and against a decision in life based on all the previous times we've faced a similar situation. Instead, the mind does something much more elegant: It weighs the *emotional* bottom line from those previous experiences and delivers the answer to us in a hunch, a gut feeling.

Goleman then goes on to say:

> The notion that there is "pure thought," rationality devoid of feeling, is a fiction, an illusion based on inattention of the subtle moods that follow us through the day. We have feelings about everything we do, think about, imagine, remember. Thought and feeling are inextricably woven together.[3]

This notion of thought and feeling being "inextricably woven together" can be highly problematic for some technical or process-oriented individuals. First, it defies their belief that numbers and sequences are more important than emotions. Second, they see the left-brain activities of analysis, process, and steps as much more concrete, orderly, and "real." Hopefully, Goleman's and others' work, as well as our rapidly changing understanding of how the brain works, will begin to ease some of those fears—for what we are learn-ing is how *fundamental emotions are to effective decision making.*

Many businesspeople struggle with the importance of self-awareness because in order to become self-aware, we must confront our feelings—about ourselves and others. We must take time to stop and reflect. For some, this can be a frightening experience because when feeling is confronted, when dealing with emotion-ally charged situations, these businesspeople may not even know *what to name* an emotion. Furthermore, what if I learn something about myself that I don't like? As the King of Siam once said, "Tis a puzzlement."

Why Is Self-Awareness Important in Business?

Up to this point, we've been speaking about establishing powerful business relationships, but we have not as yet focused on what is perhaps the most critical relationship of them all—*the relationship with oneself.* Bill George, former CEO of Medtronics, a manufacturer of medical devices, argues that unless people know themselves and their values, they cannot effectively lead others. During his tenure at Medtronics (1991–2001), the company's market capitalization went from $1 billion to $60 billion, and the share price rocketed 1,800 per-cent from 1993 to 2000. Clearly, George had experienced firsthand what was required to lead a high-performing company. In an inter-view with the Public Broadcast System (PBS) in 2007, he said:

> Leaders, first of all, have to develop themselves. And the leaders that I've seen who have failed, have failed to lead themselves. . . . They aren't well grounded. And I think staying grounded is one of the hardest tasks any leader has to do. . . . You're grounded in your values. You know what you believe. And if you get pressure from the outside world to do this, do that, you say no. I know what I believe.[4]

This grounding comes from knowing our values and ourselves.

Dee Hock, ex-CEO of Visa International, at one point grew his firm to the single largest business in the world, and he agrees with George, saying:

> The first and paramount responsibility of anyone who purports to manage is to manage self—one's own integrity, character, ethics, knowledge, wisdom, temperament, words, and acts. It is a never-ending, difficult, oft-shunned task. The reason is not complicated. It is ignored precisely because it is incredibly more difficult than prescribing and controlling the behavior of others.
>
> Without exceptional self management, few are fit for authority, no matter how much they acquire. In truth, the more authority they acquire, the more dangerous they become. The management of self should have half our time and the best of our ability. In the process, the ethical, moral, and spiritual elements of managing self are inescapable.[5]

Although Western business schools have almost solely emphasized the left-brain analytical skills, process tools, and logic, this is beginning to change. More and more people—both academics and business leaders—are beginning to understand that emotional intelligence, which includes self-awareness, may be the real key to a leader's success. Much of that shift in perspective comes from both exciting research in the field of neuroscience and from work by Goleman and many others. Goleman, though, argues the data suggest "that the importance of emotional intelligence increases the higher you go in the organization." He also goes on to say, *"[F]or star performance in all jobs, in every field, emotional intelligence is twice as important as purely cognitive abilities"* [italics added].[6]

This change of perspective regarding the importance of emotional intelligence is nowhere more apparent than in the changes that are occurring at Harvard Business School. Long known for its rigorous case-analysis method, which has been adopted by many other business schools, Harvard has begun implementing new ways of approaching leadership development. We see this most recently in Bill George's article, "Leadership Starts with Self-Awareness," written for the *Minneapolis Star Tribune* on February 26, 2012:

> Last week I served as faculty chair for Harvard Business School's new executive course, "Authentic Leadership Development." Sixty-four executives from 60 global companies spent five intense days honing their leadership.
>
> Here's the catch: They concentrated almost entirely on leading themselves, not others.[7]

Some leading business thinkers and writers, such as Henry Mintzberg, would applaud this changing focus. Mintzberg, who has long argued that training managers with the pure left-brain approach is misguided, says in his *Managers Not MBAs*:

> [W]e need leaders with human skills, not professionals with academic credentials. In the larger organizations especially, success depends not on what the managers themselves do, as allocators of resources and makers of decisions, so much as on what they help others to do.[8]

In other words, effectiveness in many cases comes down to a manager's ability to forge strong relationships through which productivity can flow. Why won't pure analytics work? Why is the soft stuff—such as self-awareness—so critical? Mintzberg says:

> The practice of management is characterized by its ambiguity. That is why, despite its popular use, the metaphor of the conductor on the podium is wholly inappropriate (at least during performance, if not necessarily rehearsal). Most work that can be programmed in an organization need not concern its managers directly; specialists can be delegated to do it. That leaves the managers mostly with the messy stuff—the intractable problems, the complicated connections. And that is what makes the practice of management so fundamentally "soft" and why labels

such as experience, intuition, judgment, and wisdom are so commonly used for it. Here is how a successful manager at a major airline described her MBA husband to me: "He has the technique, thinks he knows best. But he is frustrated because he doesn't understand the complexities and the politics. He thinks he has the answers but is frustrated by being unable to do anything about it." He never learned management in the business school.[9]

How Do We Become More Self-Aware?

If we haven't had an opportunity to learn these skills in business school, how can we learn to be more self-aware? How can we become more self-aware in such a way that we become more—not less—confident about ourselves?

Mintzberg felt so strongly about the shortcomings of traditional MBA programs that he founded his own business school, the International Masters in Practicing Management (IMPM). He required that all people applying to his program have 5–10 years of management experience. The IMPM begins with two weeks on *reflective thinking*, which includes focused meditation, asking hard questions about one's self, taking feedback from others, and acting on one's insights. Mintzberg's thesis is simple, that "[r]eflection without action is passive; action without reflection is thoughtless."[10] As Mintzberg says:

> To develop a reflective turn of mind, the participants focus on themselves, their work, and their world, to appreciate how they think, act, and manage; how they cope with the stresses of being a manager; and how they learn from experience to become more discerning—more "critical" in the constructive sense of this word.[11]

If you received an MBA more than five years ago, think back. How would your younger self have reacted to starting business school with two weeks of self-reflection? Although Mintzberg was concerned about students' reactions to spending two weeks this way, he was pleasantly surprised at how the managers/participants reacted to the first module so strongly, saying:

> A surprising number of the participants have told us over the years that this module turned out to be a life-changing experience. Initially, this effect took me by surprise, but it should not have. Managers are terribly harassed these days. They rarely stop, even in their so-called free time. Suddenly they find themselves in a relaxed setting, free for hours on end to engage in all kinds of unexpected reflective activities, and the results can be profound. Near the end of the second cycle, a participant polled her classmates as to whether the IMPM had been a life-changing experience. All but one said yes (the one was not *yet* sure!) and most pointed to the opening module [on reflection, which promoted self-awareness].
>
> We were nervous the first time we ran this module, not only because the program was so new but also because we had no precedent for running two weeks of reflection for managers. Now, with several years' experience behind us, we can only wonder why that should have been. Contemporary managers have a great deal of time *not* to reflect. By beginning with reflection, the IMPM sets a tone for developing more thoughtful, more balanced, and wiser managers.[12]

Not only did the managers see the self-reflective module as life-changing, but many of them continued to schedule time for reflection when they returned to their companies, usually coming in early to consider solutions to issues they were facing. It seems like such a simple thing, but ask yourself: How often do you find reflective time in your business life? What would you give for 30 minutes of such time? Twenty? Ten? It's there if you take it, as are the results.

Writing in 1994 in their book, *Competing for the Future: Breakthrough Strategies for Seizing Control of Your Industry and*

Creating the Markets of Tomorrow, Gary Hamel and C. K. Prahalad describe the driven thoughtless nature of much management, saying, "[T]he urgent drives out the important; the future goes largely unexplored; and the capacity to act, rather than the capacity to think and imagine, becomes the sole measure of leadership."[13] This quotation should give pause to experienced managers. We have all been there.

It is through reflection that we come to both a greater knowledge of self—who we are—and greater effectiveness in solving our business challenges.

Self-Awareness Arises from Feedback from Others

Self-awareness begins with a desire to know who you are and what you want. As Nancy Barry, CEO of Women's World Banking, said in a speech to businesspeople: "Take the time to get to know yourself and find your passion. Look inside, to find your power, your purpose. If you find and go with this flow, you will make a difference in our world—and you will find joy in the journey."[14]

The primary way to know yourself is to proactively seek, listen to, and reflect on feedback from others. Regularly debrief interactions and projects. Conduct what the U.S. Army calls "after-action reviews." What did I do that I should keep doing? What was not helpful and I should stop doing? What should I start doing? Do differently? Seek useful feedback—something you can act on—*not judgments or critiques*, which often tell you what didn't work but not what you can do to improve your approach. The goal is to become good at practicing what Chris Argyris calls "double-loop learning," in which you focus not solely on solving the problem out there (the single loop) but also by looking at yourself and considering to what, if any, extent your behavior may be causing the very problem you're trying to solve (the second loop).[15]

Another reason to develop self-awareness is so that you can better understand and appreciate others. As Bill George, ex-CEO of Medtronics, says, "Without being aware of your vulnerabilities, fears, and longings, it is hard to empathize with others who are experiencing similar feelings."[16] This point shows once again how intertwined are the keys in this book, how when you pull one key, others move with it.

In Your Search for Self-Awareness, Beware Your Drunken Monkey

The concept of the drunken monkey comes from Buddha's concept of the "monkey mind." The monkey is that little voice in your head that is always chattering, trying to get your attention, distracting you, making you worry about things out of your control. It's the conversations you can have with yourself. Check it out. Look at your watch, and stop and listen to your monkey for 60 seconds. What did you hear? "What is it talking about? Is it nuts? What monkey?" Or, "I thought I was nuts. I have a whole bunch of monkeys talking to me!" The monkey becomes loudest when we are frightened or worried, imagining all the things that could go wrong—that we're likely to screw up. We call it a drunken monkey because sometimes it's out of control. The drunken monkey is so loud that sometimes we can't even hear what another person is saying. In highly charged situations especially, we often spend more time talking with our-selves—*listening to our own drunken monkey*—than listening to the true feedback and thoughts of others.

For example, your friend says, "I hate to tell you this . . ." and before he even says the next word, you're already thinking, "Oh, man, here it comes! What has he . . . ?" You know the story. It's what happens when someone yells at us, "You may have been listening, but you didn't hear me." Listening to our monkey can limit both our understanding of the situation and the learning necessary to improve ourselves and our relationships. The conversations we have with ourselves profoundly affect what we hear other people say.

As a result of our drunken monkey, we frequently misinterpret what others are saying. How many times have you misinterpreted a statement and then acted under the wrong assumptions? Without getting too psychological, the way our brains are wired—with our insecurities and lack of self-awareness—can sometimes create bad situations where none exist. The key, then, is to be self-aware and to use the feedback that others are giving you while being extremely careful that the feedback you hear is actually what the other person is saying and not your drunken monkey screaming at you.

As we look back on our lives and careers, we can see how this insight would have saved us from much self-created pain. Lack of self-awareness—and its sometimes attendant inability to understand others—can do you much damage, personally and professionally. Being self-aware not only will make you more effective in your business relationships, but it also will make many aspects of your life easier and ultimately more fulfilling.

POINTS TO REMEMBER

Overview

>> The most important relationship in business is the one we have with ourselves. By examining our own strengths and weaknesses objectively, we are able to identify opportunities that can improve our relationships with others. This emotional intelligence is a primary driver of the quality of business relationships we have with other individuals, teams, and organizations.

>> Thoughts and feelings are inextricably woven together. If our emotions affect the decisions we all make, it is important for each of us to be in tune with and understand the impact of the relationship we have with ourselves.

For Individuals

>> Our self-awareness, as described by Daniel Goleman, includes
  ○ Emotional awareness
  ○ Accurate self-assessment
  ○ Self-confidence

>> Try this: Come into the office very early some morning and do not check your messages and e-mails—don't get pulled into the tornado. Simply consider the largest problem you are currently facing, and concentrate on that. Determine some ways that you might solve it. If this approach works (and we suggest you try it at least three times), make it a regular part of your day.

>> Determine what your drunken monkey makes you do. How do you act differently when under stress? What kinds of actions do you wish you wouldn't do? If you think back, where has your drunken monkey led you in the wrong direction? Once you have even a small handle on your drunken monkey, start controlling it. Breathe before you speak or acknowledge what you are feeling. If your monkey gets out, apologize. Your business life might change.

For Teams

>> After your next three projects, conduct *after-action reviews.* Have the group ask itself:
  ◦ "What did I do that I should keep doing?"
  ◦ "What was not helpful and I should stop doing?"
  ◦ "What should I start doing?"
  ◦ "What should I do differently?"

>> Make sure that everyone on your team understands the rules. Start by asking yourself the questions, and then ask the group for useful feedback—something you can act on—*not judgments or critiques*—which often tell you what didn't work but not what you can do to adapt your approach.

 For Organizations

>> Self-awareness arises from soliciting and using feedback of others. The same holds true on an organizational level as well. The thoughts and attitudes of both employees and customers can shape the culture of an organization. The best companies, though, have an ability to use that internal and external chatter to make modifications on the fly.

>> It is important to create a business culture in which it is safe to share contrary opinions.

>> What information does your company currently obtain from its employees (in the form of surveys, questionnaires, or reviews) that can reveal some insight into known problems or issues? Does the company also collect ideas that might help the organization thrive?

>> Does your company collect and use the feedback of its customers? If so, is that feedback being used to continuously improve the company's products, services, and/or customer experience?

NOTES

A Review of the Five Keys

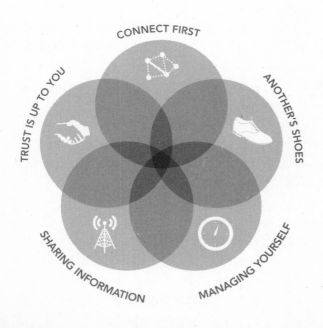

CONNECT FIRST

ANOTHER'S SHOES

TRUST IS UP TO YOU

SHARING INFORMATION

MANAGING YOURSELF

We've been examining five practices relationship masters use to establish powerful business relationships, because we know that by using some of these practices you, too, can continue to grow and thrive. As Peter Rouse says, "There is no problem that is not, at one level or another, a relationship problem. There are few joys that are not based in or shared through relationships."[1]

Unfortunately, much of business in the western world still worships in the land of the hard, the analytical, the quantifiable, the traditional means of cost-justifying investments. This means that while there are many who will praise the idea of business relationships to the skies, they may balk when they are asked to make an investment to repair or build a better relationship—whether internally or with large customers, a partner firm, or a critical supplier. They balk because they cannot determine a quantifiable return. Let's return to W. Edwards Deming, who in 1950 provided a great insight into this numerical fixation when he said, "[H]e that would run his company on visible figures alone will in time have neither company nor figures."[2]

As we have seen, those who focus solely on the analytical often have a difficult time connecting with their colleagues, customers, and suppliers. As James A. Autry, author of *Love and Profit: The Art of Caring Leadership,* says:

No matter what anyone tells you, when you lose business, it's almost *always* a relationship problem. Good relationships and personal connections can come only when you abandon the patterned thinking and language of business. Most business language tries to communicate the intellectual technicalities of business, and is somewhat effective in doing so, but this language has no place in the vocabulary of feelings and ideas that make up the spirit of business.[3]

It is this spirit of business that we have focused on—how many people, closely working together, can establish relationships and common goals and produce a great deal more than they could individually. This is what we call *thriving*.

By discussing five interconnected keys to establishing more powerful business relationships, we have shown repeatedly that there is no one "right" way to build these relationships. We'll review the five keys and then provide you with the sorts of questions you need to reflect on and answer for yourself in order to be effective in each of the practices.

Key #1: Connect First; Then Focus on Task—In Review

Developing relationships requires that you learn by listening to another person. You want to learn about who that person is, what he or she wants, and what he or she is hoping to achieve. As Maribeth Kuzmeski, author of *The Connectors: How the World's Most Successful Businesspeople Build Relationships and Win Clients for Life,* says:

> The key determinant at the top of all business strategies, talents, and expertise is the ability to connect with people on a meaningful level—one that produces quality associations and profitable business relationships. In essence, it is how we make others feel within the connections that we have that brings the success we desire.[4]

Once the connection is partially made, one of the ways the relationship can then be developed is by considering which of the social currencies the person values. In addition, as Joan Holmes says, "If you listen carefully, you show the other person to whom you're listening a profound respect. That makes a relationship work."[5]

Take Time to Reflect

What sorts of questions do you need to ask to determine the quality of connectedness? Here are some worth considering:

Which relationships are you in where something feels "off"?

>> Why is that?

>> What specific data do you have that lead you to believe that something is off?

>> What is missing for you?

>> Is there something incomplete in your history with this person?

>> What new connections might need to be established with that person or those persons?

>> Have you confirmed that the other person(s) is feeling the same way? If not, could you find a way to casually check things out?

>> What is admirable about the other person? Have you recognized their contribution?

Think about a time when a relationship problem got in the way of accomplishing an important task or goal.

>> What was the impact?

>> Did the relationship problem get resolved?

>> What could you do to avoid a similar situation in the future?

What did you do to establish the appropriate level of relationship before you began a recent project or task?

>> How did that work?

>> How did you know?

>> What difference did it make?

>> What might you do differently next time?

> **Even when there is a strong level of relationship, stress, deadlines, long hours, and roadblocks also can challenge the relationship.**
>
> » What can be done to keep the relationship intact?
>
> » How might using some of the techniques below help minimize relationship challenges during times of stress?
>
> • Clear, supportive communication?
>
> • Authentic apologies?
>
> • Acknowledging others?
>
> • Allowing people to say what they have to say without the other taking it personally and becoming defensive?

Key #2: Walking in Someone Else's Shoes—In Review

The ability to demonstrate empathy is one way to establish and strengthen your connection with another person. But there's nothing easy about it. You have to step outside yourself and determine where the other person is coming from. As Bruce Barnes, former CIO, says:

> Assuming that you have already identified the solid targets with whom effective relationships need to be built, the subsequent "building process" is predicated on first figuring out what is meaningful to those other parties in terms of their goals and aspirations. It also means figuring out what kind of connection they want with you, too, in order for them to feel comfortable to achieving that goal with you.
>
> In shaping those discussions, I always fall back to my definition of a word that I find most people do not understand ... "partner." To my way of thinking, true partnership is defined by finding an equitable balance of sharing along five different dimensions, i.e., ongoing costs, resulting profits, encountered risk, associated information, and required resources. Anything

less is not a "partnership." Achieving a balance across those elements helps to assure a collective vision of winning ... "all in together" ... which is a solid foundation for a great relationship.[6]

On its surface, partnership seems an easy thing to accomplish. Why is it such a challenge for some businesspeople? The greatest challenge, as Joan Holmes explains, is learning how to subsume your own ego and open yourself to the other person. As she says:

I don't see many people with the openness and the willingness to listen to who the other person is. Not just what the person is saying, but who are they? Because that is a deeper listening, isn't it? To do that, you really have to open yourself and be authentically interested. I see a lot of people who want to share their opinions early on—like "let me tell you about my point of view for the last thirty years." People's focus is more on themselves than on the person with whom they are talking. If you are talking with someone and you're still more interested in yourself, you are more in your head than available to the other person. Know that there's no good that comes out of being in your head. It creates distance, and it creates dissonance in what could be a phenomenal relationship.[7]

Take Time to Reflect
What sorts of questions do you need to ask to determine whether you have truly walked in the other person's shoes?

Do you find yourself assuming that you know what others really want? Really need?
>> When have you been wrong in your assumption?
>> What happened as a result?
>> What steps could you take to keep from assuming too quickly in the future?

What do you do to understand your customers' (or colleagues' or suppliers') needs, requirements, and wish lists?

>> How has that worked?

>> What should you consider doing that you haven't done to learn their true needs, requirements, and wish lists?

>> How frequently do you need to keep asking them if any of these needs, requirements, and lists have changed?

Once you have done everything you know to do to understand the needs of others, how do you make sure that you have fully understood?

>> What could you do that you haven't tried?

>> If you cannot meet their needs, do you say so honestly?

>> What was the impact on the relationship of doing that?

>> What do you do to ensure that those needs are translated for others who might need this information?

Do you know what keeps your key relationships "up at night"?

>> Your company's executives?

>> Your boss?

>> That colleague who is driving you crazy?

>> The person you should be working with but keep avoiding?

Key #3: Whether People Trust You Is Often up to You—In Review

After you have learned who the other person is, what he or she is trying to achieve, and how he or she would like to work with you, there can be a sale, an agreement, or a deal, and with the agreement will come certain commitments. These commitments may be ship dates or payment dates or complete order loads or whatever, but the continued health of the business relationship depends on whether you live up to these commitments. This is not to say that you won't sometimes get it wrong, but if you do, it is far better to have established trust over time because then you have chits you can use to solve those missteps.

Take Time to Reflect

What sorts of questions do you need to ask to determine whether you have established trust in your relationships?

> **How do you know if someone trusts you?**

> **What happened that caused you to lose trust in someone you had to work with?**
> - ≫ What did you do as a result?
> - ≫ What did you do to get the relationship back on track?

> **Do you feel that people generally trust you?**
> - ≫ What evidence do you have that your perceptions are correct?
> - ≫ Have you ever had a colleague act surprised by your behavior?
> - ≫ In that case, what expectation did they have of you that you didn't meet?

> **Do you trust yourself?**

To what extent are you reluctant to trust others because you've gotten burned in the past?

>> What have you tried to do to overcome that reluctance?

>> How has that worked?

>> What could you do differently going forward?

When have you let people down?

>> What happened?

>> How did you find out?

>> What did you do to repair the situation?

>> How successful were you in repairing it?

>> Did your solution fully restore their trust in you?

To what extent do you keep your word?

>> Follow-through?

>> Keep confidences?

>> Resist asserting things for which you lack credible evidence?

>> Tell the truth?

Do you acknowledge when you have made a mistake or been out of integrity?

>> How has that worked for you?

>> What did you learn about yourself?

Key #4: Sharing Information to Increase Personal Power—In Review

To play full out in business, you need to be genuinely interested in those with whom you have business relationships. One of the ways you can demonstrate such caring is by continually recognizing the good points in their opinions and sharing information that may help them to do *their* work more effectively. The best relationship managers we know argue that sharing information actually increases their personal power and builds empowering business relationships.

Almost all the executives we spoke with said that better decisions get made when teams are working together and when people hoard neither their opinions nor their information. The best leaders will encourage those who are shy about putting forth their opinions. They solicit the shy person's opinions, listen respectfully, and know that they have thereby increased the number of possible solutions.

Here Doug Renfro, president of Renfro Foods, speaks about teams and product development:

> By having a collaborative discussion, you'll end up with a better product every time. I've got pride like everybody else, but you've got to acknowledge that the result of these group discussions is always better than what I come up with on my own. I think when you are all in the same room, it is like a lab. I just don't believe [that] one person tends to have the best ideas.[8]

To arrive at the best idea, it's more effective to share information and opinions and to have the team determine the best solution. And such sharing increases the connection, the empathy, and the trust in your business relationships.

Take Time to Reflect

What sorts of questions do you need to ask to determine whether you are effective at sharing information in your relationships?

How do you feel when you are kept out of the loop?

How do you feel when you are in the loop and have the information that you want or need to make good decisions?

>> Do your colleagues know what information you like to have or need to have and in what format?

>> How/when do your colleagues want to be communicated with?

What communication tools are available to you?

>> Which of those tools work best for:

- Information sharing?
- Problem solving?
- Collaboration?

>> What could you do to make more effective use of these tools?

>> What information are you, your employees, your colleagues, and/or your team craving?

>> How do your colleagues' views compare with yours?

>> Are you willing to work with them to create better processes for sharing information?

Are you "listening for" what information needs to be shared in each meeting or discussion?

>> What are the issues?

>> What has been decided and why?

>> Who needs to know?

Do you have internal communication systems?

>> Are you someone who can listen objectively to feedback and ideas from every level in the company?

- With which level or area in the company do you have the most difficulty communicating?
- Why do you think that is?
- Why do they think that is?

Have you connected and empathized with team members to best facilitate the sharing of information?

>> What have you done?

Key #5: Manage Yourself Before You Manage Others—In Review

There is a consensus growing among business leaders that before you can effectively manage another person, you have to know yourself. And the higher you go in the organization and the more complex the job, the greater is the degree of self-awareness required. This self-awareness includes being aware of the impact of the chatter of your monkey mind. To help specifically with this, we are seeing more and more businesspeople exercising, meditating, and practicing yoga. We also see more people proactively soliciting feedback about their impact on others. They want to know themselves more completely so that they can be more effective as leaders.

What does greater self-awareness allow? It promotes greater self-management. As our colleague Nicholas Wolfson says:

The one thing that you can manage is your attitude. It's very hard to manage your emotions—they come and they go. You may suddenly find yourself afraid for no particular reason, or you may find yourself ecstatic for no particular reason. Feelings are like weather. But your attitude you can manage. It's like your commitments. It's like what you stand for; you have a say in that always. So you can stand for possibility. You walk in the room, and my commitment is that I don't know how this damn thing is going to turn out, but I'm committed. That great possibility is present.[9]

Take Time to Reflect

What sorts of questions do you need to ask to determine whether you know yourself well?

> **Are you able to name how you're feeling about most situations?**

> **To what extent are you usually able to clearly see situations?**
>
> » To what extent do you find your interpretations of a situation vastly different from those of others in or observing the situation?
>
> » When were you particularly effective in determining what was really happening?
>
> » When were you not?

> **To what extent do your fears and insecurities about yourself:**
>
> » Affect your relationship with others?
>
> » Affect your overall effectiveness?
>
> » Influence what you might do differently going forward to remedy this?

To what extent does your drunken monkey interfere with your ability to be effective?

>> With communication, management?

>> What changes do you need to make in your life to support your growing and thriving?

>> What objections, if any, do you have to take time during your day to reflect?

>> Are you willing to include your feelings when you make a decision?

>> How can you strengthen your ability to reflect:

- About your relationships?
- About your approach to doing your job?
- About your personal information-sharing strategy?

>> What difference would it make in your work and life if you optimized your relationships?

So these are five keys to powerful business relationships that we have examined and five lists of self-reflective questions. All will help you to develop and maintain the business relations on which your success and your firm's success depend. Let Domonic Biggi, vice president of Beaverton Foods, conclude with some words to live by:

Life has a way of humbling us. That's true. Every time I find myself getting a little too big, somebody throws a little piece of humble pie at me, and that's fine. You get too big, you fall big. I have a low threshold for pain. Stay humble, keep working hard, keep moving forward and be good to the people around you.[10]

A farmer friend once said that in his world, "[g]reen is growing, and ripe means it's ready to rot." May you and your business always "be green" and continue to grow and thrive.

PART 3

Virtual Relationships and the Five Keys

Our increasing reliance on technology to develop and manage virtual relationships presents some profound challenges. While technology can speed things up, that speed can also muddle our message and ultimately slow things down. Paying attention to the five keys may save you time and unnecessary digital frustration.

Applying the Five Keys to Virtual Relationships

Throughout this book we have been talking about five keys to creating and sustaining powerful, empowering business relationships. At the heart of these keys is our ability to connect and communicate. As a wise man once told one of us, connections are the harness that pulls your wagon. Because we exist in this web of relationships spun together through communication, we believe that the ability to share our meaning—our message—is a core business competency.

Applying the five keys to virtual relationships offers some major challenges. For example, we will be dealing with digital platforms as they exist at the time of this writing. While we recognize these platforms will change, we believe that the *Five Keys* will apply to whatever new platforms come along. A second challenge is that, in our experience, only a very few businesspeople work to determine whether the message they sent was the message their recipient received—they simply assume that it was. It seems as if most businesspeople dramatically underestimate the skill—and the time—required to communicate effectively. As George Bernard Shaw supposedly once said, "The single biggest problem in communication is the illusion that it has taken place."[1] And James Thurber stated it more emphatically, saying, "Precision of communication is important, more important than ever, in our era of hair trigger balances, when a false or misunderstood word may create as much disaster as a sudden thoughtless act."[2]

To understand what we mean, think of a time when you thought that you had communicated your message clearly in an e-mail, only to spend hours later trying to straighten out a huge misunderstanding. It's an almost universal experience.

Although virtual communication can sometimes be challenging even with our closest friends, communicating virtually in business can exponentially complicate things—and cost both time and money. Why is this? In friendships, trust has been earned, and our shared experiences have enabled us to create a shared context within which we can easily understand and influence one another. We share power *and* influence. When we have questions, we ask. When we are irritated, we say so.

In business, the communication and relationship contexts are often quite different. We frequently work with people who have more or less *positional power* than we do (e.g., our bosses or our direct reports). We also work with people with whom we may have little or no experience or trust. Where our friends often know us well enough that they can sometimes fill in our words and meaning in a digital communication, most business colleagues cannot. Nor will they necessarily give us the benefit of the doubt.

What this lack of experience and trust means is that most digital business communication generally needs to be *far more precise* than when communicating with friends. Our meaning in our message needs to be clear, and we must follow up to make certain that what we intended to communicate was actually what was heard. The common phrase "you know what I mean" seldom works in business. Our casual (some would call it sloppy) communication style that works with friends often backfires at work where words matter—in getting things done, avoiding legal problems, and building powerful, empowering relationships.

To make matters more difficult, the tools we use to communicate in business settings have changed drastically. Until about 15 years ago, business relationships were bound together primarily through letters, written memos, over the phone, and in face-to-face interactions. Business writing was deliberate, well-thought-out, and often much more structured than the same sort of communication these days. Generally speaking, there was *time* to process reactions and emotions between interactions. Audiences were also usually more defined in terms of age, gender, and cultural background. We had a better idea of what to expect from whom when we communicated.

The advent of the digital age has provided new ways to communicate instantaneously to much broader audiences. Now we can have continuous, simultaneous, virtual relationships with colleagues around the globe, often with people whom we have never met or spoken with. This offers massive communication opportunities but also introduces huge new communication challenges when it comes to creating business relationships. In digital interactions, we can sometimes receive multiple pieces of feedback before we have even processed the receiver's first response. Sometimes we don't have time to catch our breath—or even know what we think—before the conversation moves on. Because we can tweet, send videos and links to archival data, the emotional impact of the message is stronger and much more far-reaching than ever before. Our purpose in this *virtual relationships* section is not to critique the various digital platforms but rather to demonstrate ways that you might apply the keys to digital communication so as *to increase the power* of your virtual relationships. After a short examination of specific challenges in digital communication, we will look at each key to see how it might be used to promote and strengthen your virtual business relationships.

Relationship Challenges in Digital Communication

The first challenge is a conundrum we've seen many times: businesspeople who communicate effectively face-to-face but who often struggle to write the most basic message clearly. They have difficulties with focus, with logical flow, or with word choice, even when they communicate about something they know well. The end result is that poor writing buries their point.

How many e-mails have you received, for example, where you think that you know the author's meaning but aren't quite sure? In any communication, we need a clear sense of who the audience is and what they are expecting. In digital written communication, because we have only words to make our point, it is particularly critical that we use the precise words we need. As Mark Twain once said, "The difference between the right word and the almost right word is the difference between lightning and the lightning bug."[3] This goes in spades for digital communication.

Second, with these written communications, we must ensure that the reader has the proper context to understand our message. This challenge doesn't sound insurmountable, but in face-to-face communication, the recipient has our body language and tonal messages to provide more communication context. When we say something intended to be humorous face-to-face, the recipient has contextual guides to know what we mean. But when we try to be humorous in digital communication, our attempts may be taken as our true opinion, which can create all sorts of problems. Some people will try to use emoticons (e.g., smiley faces) to nuance the humor, but those too can be easily misunderstood. Until every computer user has a camera (and that day is fast approaching), we need to pay particular care when using humor if we want to pre-serve our business relationships.

Third, there is the challenge of the speed of digital communica-tion and how it affects the psychology of the Internet. David Shipley and Will Schwalbe, in their *Send: The Essential Guide to Email for Office and Home*, explain the problem this way:

> We ... email fast—inevitably too fast.... [T]he speed of email doesn't just make it easier to lose our cool—it actually eggs us on. On email, people aren't quite themselves: they are angrier,

less sympathetic, less aware, more easily wounded, even more gossipy and duplicitous. Email has a tendency to encourage the lesser angels of our nature.[4]

Often we feel compelled to communicate too quickly online. In some cases it is the instantaneous nature of the communication, but it also is a matter of the expectations of those waiting for us to communicate/reply, which can easily spur us on to communicate even more quickly. In an article that appeared in 2010 in the *Manchester (England) Evening News*, the writer describes a study conducted by Telewest Business among 1,400 British businesspeople about how quickly they expect a response from digital communications. The author describes the study's findings by saying:

> The survey . . . suggests that almost one-half of UK office workers would consider it rude not to have received a reply to an email within a morning. And 5 percent of people would consider it rude if they had not received an email response *within five minutes of sending it* [these people must live a life of ongoing disappointment—our comment and emphasis]. The survey claims that two out of every five people would expect a response to a text message within an hour before considering it rude, and almost a quarter of the people questioned expect a response within five minutes to an instant message[5] [italics added].

More recent research shows similar results. A lecturer from the University of Glasgow revealed in 2008 that e-mail users fall into three basic categories: stressed, driven, and relaxed. The 34 percent who were "stressed" felt overwhelmed by the number of messages sent to them each day, checking their inbox between *30 and 40 times per hour*. Perhaps more alarming than the compulsory inbox monitoring were their response times. "On average, people waited only one minute and 44 seconds before acting upon a new email notification; however, two thirds of alerts got a reaction within six seconds, or faster than letting the phone ring three times."[6]

With a highly critical or sensitive digital communication, it is almost always better to delay our response. Why? Waiting to draft a response allows us to better analyze the sender's original message. It also allows us to review what we have written in response. A CEO we know takes a similar approach, refusing to answer a tricky or problematic e-mail on her handheld device. She discovered that she was much more likely to get hooked—to rush an ineffective reply—if she answered immediately. Her rule now is to reply to such an e-mail only when she can see it on her office laptop screen. When she does that, she is not speed reading, grasping only a few loaded words. On the larger screen, she can see the words and meaning more clearly. It may be, as she says, that she simply communicates more effectively when she has more time to think about the initial e-mail to which she is replying. Whatever the reason, she is convinced that her approach makes her responses clearer and more helpful. Few businesspeople we know have such communication strategies because most of us hate to slow things down. But clarity in relationships demands regaining the concentration the Internet undercuts.

The time it takes to respond to digital communications is shaped by two factors: the type of platform and the type of relationship between the users. Up to this point, we have focused primarily on e-mail (a targeted distribution platform) in the work environment (where at least some prior type of relationship between correspondents has probably been established). Larger broadcast platforms such as Facebook can create a much different expectation in response times, especially considering the complex number of relationship types that exist in a many-to-many social platform.

The same can typically be said for Twitter, the hugely popular social networking platform that allows users to send a 140-character note (called a *tweet*) to keep their "followers" informed about where they are and what they are doing. A tweet, by default, is public—and, more important, usually only targeted to the writer's "followers." If e-mail is the online equivalent of having a conversation with someone, Twitter is the digital version of talking to yourself and hoping that someone is close enough to hear you and then decide to start a conversation with you.

That said, Twitter offers ways for its users to correspond more directly in a one-on-one setting—known as a *reply*. Users tagged in a tweet are notified that they have been mentioned and can chose to reply back or ignore it. On an individual level, this is a very useful service. On a large scale—such as that of, say, Nike's or Whole Foods' Twitter accounts—following up with thousands of replies an hour can turn into quite an undertaking, which leads us back to our original point: expectations of response time.

Consumers overwhelmingly expect brands—particularly ones with large, active online presences—to respond to them almost immediately. A study conducted by Edison Research stated: "Among those respondents who have ever attempted to contact a brand, product, or company through social media for customer support, 57 percent expect the same response time at night and on weekends as during normal business hours." Even worse, "24 percent of American Internet users ages 12+ who have contacted a brand in social media *expect a reply within 30 minutes, regardless of when the contact was made*"[7] [italics added]. So it pays—at least in some ways—to have employees at 2:00 a.m. poised to respond to consumer questions.

To emphasize Shipley and Schwalbe's point about the dangers of hastened communication, Daniel Goleman, author of *Social Intelligence*, says that e-mail (and other Internet communication platforms) causes our fourth challenge—known as the "online disinhibition effect," which psychologists apply to the many ways people behave with less restraint in cyberspace.[8] In other words, when we are communicating over the Internet, we are sometimes not ourselves (or maybe too much ourselves!). In fact, disinhibition can release our drunken monkey (Key #5) and prevent us from considering the feelings of others (Key #2). It's all a part of the speed, ease, and urgency of online communication. So, before hitting SEND, it's wise to read and perhaps reread what we've written to try to see it from the recipient's viewpoint. This is not easy—it requires creating some distance between ourselves and our words.

These four main challenges of digital communication—poor writing skills, words without context, speed without clarity, and the online disinhibition effect—can profoundly affect our business relationships. Now let's see how we can use the five keys to avoid those problems.

Key #1: Connect First; Then Focus on Task

Although counterintuitive to the speedy response that digital platforms seem to require of us, it makes good business sense to take the time to practice our first key in our digital communications: *Connect First; Then Focus on Task.* Connecting first helps us to develop empowering relationships by creating more and more context at every interaction point. Over time, these interactions can create new and real relationships that affect you and the way your company does business. You can see it most easily in the e-mails of world-class customer-service people, a few of whom we've been lucky enough to know. They almost always preface their digital communications with a personal note authentically recognizing the receiver—little things like, "What have you been up to?" "How's your business?" or "How are you doing after your illness?" We can think of numerous gifted customer-service people who have maintained years of digital communication with targeted customer executive contacts. We've seen customer executives invite those line workers to a business meeting so that the executive can finally meet them. It doesn't take much effort, but by letting the recipient know that we are thinking about him or her, we've established a connection that humanizes the message and prepares that person to listen.

One digital observer said that firms that succeed with online communications do so not by advertising and selling their products but by "engaging with their followers and giving them valuable information."[9] Consider JetBlue Airlines, which has its customer service on Twitter 24/7. The airline defines its service goal by say-ing, "Our goal would be to make ourselves available, help whenever possible, and show that our brand is built by real people who care about our customers."[10] The best business tweets forge empowering customer relationships.

Another corporate success story on Twitter is Whole Foods, with over 2.5 million followers. Although it must be very tempt-ing to push product, one observer said, "[T]hey didn't get that many followers by spamming. [Instead, they are] … sharing recipes, replying [to comments], and retweeting."[11]

The benefits of humanizing our digital correspondence were most recently proven on a large scale by the e-mail subject-line testing performed by the Obama campaign during its 2012 fund-raising efforts. Over the course of the presidential race, a team of 20 writers tested e-mail subject lines ranging from "Join Me for Dinner" to "It doesn't have to be this way" to "Wow." The result? A majority of the $690 million raised by Obama for America came through direct e-mail efforts, a list 13 million subscribers strong. The top-performing subject lines were "Hey" (amount not dis-closed), followed by "I will be outspent" ($2.5 million raised)[12] and "Some scary numbers" ($1,941,379).[13] The Obama campaign shifted away from corporate-speak subject lines to create at least the perception of a more intimate relationship with recipients. The subject-line approach paid off. In politics, as in business, it doesn't pay to leave millions lying on the table.

Key #2: Learn by Walking in Another's Shoes

We spoke earlier in this book about the dangers of not under-standing our audience—not stepping into their shoes before we communicate. What can happen when we forego putting ourselves in the shoes of our audience—when our online communication is faster than our common sense? Perhaps the classic example of disas-trous digital communication comes from Chas Newkey-Burden's

Great Email Disasters, in which he tells the story of Jenny Amner, a secretary at a British financial services firm. Amner had gone to lunch with her boss, Richard Phillips, and had inadvertently spilled ketchup on Phillips' trousers. Let Newkey-Burden tell the rest of the story:

> [Phillips] ... wrote an email to ... [Amner] demanding [that] she pay for the bill to remove the ketchup stain. With the sub- ject line "Ketchup trousers," his email read: "Hi Jenny, I went to a dry cleaners at lunch and they said it would cost £4 to remove ketchup stains. If you cd let me have the cash today, that wd be much appreciated. Thanks Richard."[14]

When secretary Amner did not reply immediately, Phillips fol- lowed up, leaving a Post-It note on her desk, reminding her of his request for the £4. However, Mrs. Amner had been slow in responding to his email because she had been off work following the death of her mother, Polly.

On returning to work, the grieving Mrs. Amner saw red when she found Phillips's email and follow-up note. She replied to her boss's email with the following stinging message: "I must apologise for not getting back to you straight away, but due to my mother's sudden illness, death and funeral, I have had more pressing issues than your £4.

"I apologise again for accidentally getting a few splashes of ketchup on your trousers. Obviously, your financial need as a senior associate is greater than mine as a mere secretary.... should you feel the urgent need for the £4, it will be on my desk this afternoon, Jenny."

... Amner [then] copied all of the office's 250 staff in on her reply.... Very quickly, some of the staff at the firm forwarded the email to City contacts and ... soon the email was pinging around the financial community.... Sentiments of support for Phillips were thin on the ground. Like all good snowballing emails, the message was soon circulating around the world, and Phillips was gathering himself a reputation as a mean tightwad, while Amner was collecting supportive messages from around the world.[15]

Phillips' e-mail was very short (37 words), probably written very quickly, and certainly written without a great deal of soul-searching. And it came back to bite him big time. His personal/professional brand was damaged all because he did not take the time to walk in the shoes of his recipient.

On a broader scale, firms must understand the needs of their audience and remember that *the recipient decides the value of an online communication*, be it through tweets, e-mails, blogs, or LinkedIn notes. Before a digital message goes out, a firm had better know exactly what customers find valuable. Because if the business gets it wrong, it's easy for broadcast messages to undermine relationships.

As mentioned previously, Twitter was built to keep individuals connected. But creative businesses use Twitter to stay connected to their customers by announcing useful tools or distributing special offers to their subscribed customers. A retweet feature allows followers to resend the same tweet to their friends, which can help both to spread brand name and to easily drive more traffic to the firm's website. Twitter also makes for a great way for customers to notify companies of problems, challenges, and suggestions and for a given business to send out solutions, responses, and thank-yous in customer service.

A danger with Twitter and other platforms is that while they can help to create constant connections, your firm cannot control what people say about you as a service provider. Twitter is public and broadcast-based by default. For this reason, it is not only possible—but vitally important—to place your company in your customers' shoes by listening for tweets about your firm.

Had Rogers Communications taken this approach, it could have avoided being covered in Alicia Androich's *Marketing* piece entitled, "Rogers' Very Bad Twitter Day":

Rogers Communication … launched a social media initiative on Twitter promoting Rogers One Number, a new service that allows Rogers customers to text, talk, and video call—whether on their computer or wireless phone—using their existing Rogers wireless number.

Rogers used Twitter's "promoted tweet" functionality for the hashtag [a way of classifying a tweet topic or user or topic]: #Rogers1Number. It sat atop Twitter's trending (most popular) topics list most of the day, but Twitter posters were using the hashtag to complain about Rogers and its services. The wave of negative feedback was large enough to attract attention from news outlets such as the *Globe and Mail* and *Toronto Star*. . . . Rogers, which owns *Marketing*, began the promoted tweet campaign on Thursday night as part of an effort to raise awareness about Rogers One Number. In response, tweets ranged from personal recommendations for other service providers to commentary on the use of promoted tweets. Keith McArthur, vice president of social media at Rogers Communications, told *Marketing* on Friday afternoon that "We learn new things from our customers every day in social media. Today we're learning even more than usual."[16]

To their credit, Rogers' executives—particularly Keith McArthur—took the whole thing as a learning experience and assigned 10 Rogers employees to engage with customers as community managers or customer-service representatives. In this case, Rogers was able to improve both its services and it relationships.

The whole incident, of course, could have been avoided had Rogers walked in its customers' shoes *first* by listening to what they were saying about the brand *before* they decided to run a promotional campaign. Public platforms such as Twitter provide serious challenges to firms. If a business does not want to listen to its customers' problems, then it shouldn't use online communications platforms—especially in an advertising-only capacity. On the other hand, if a business is set up to listen, it can gain a great deal and perhaps a competitive advantage by listening to complaints and responding to them quickly. This is the double-edged sword of digital communications. We have to recognize and acknowledge our audience before moving to task. Start marketing (and then only indirect marketing) *only* after establishing a relationship and putting yourself in your customers' shoes.

Dell Computer has done a nice job of this, going so far as to segment its customers and set up numerous Twitter accounts offering different sorts of value. One expert described these accounts by saying, "Their Dell Outlet account has brought in over $2 million in sales within the first two years of operation. They had a 34 percent conversion rate for turning 'ranters' [complainers] into 'ravers' [fans]."[17] Dell understands better than most that it has to engage followers to create a relationship—before it even thinks about selling. If a firm is going to succeed on Twitter, it's critical to create the relationship by offering value. To define that value, you have to walk in the customers' shoes. If a firm starts by selling, it will be treated as a spammer and will die a digital death.

One of the most effective online sites to provide value to customers is Amazon.com. If you are interested in a book, not only can you read a description of the book, but in most cases you also can examine dozens of reader reviews, which allow you to see whether others have found value after they have read it. And woe unto those who have not written a very good book. Here is a platform where the customer has a very important voice. As an additional value, Amazon usually offers several dozen other books with topics similar to the one you are searching for. And the more you use Amazon, the better it gets at offering you similar works. It's a little scary sometimes.

Key #3: Whether People Trust You Is Often up to You

Trust, as we've already pointed out, is the foundation of empowering relationships, be they in person or digital. Earlier we suggested that trust is based on three things:

>> *Sincerity.* Do I believe that you sincerely and honestly care about my well-being?
>> *Reliability.* Can I count on you to keep your promises?
>> *Competence.* Do I believe that you are competent to do this particular task?[18]

In our digital communications, these elements are still at play. To gauge your intent or others' in writing, you might ask yourself the following kinds of questions:

>> What is the intent behind this particular communication?
>> Do you really care about me, or is there another agenda?
>> Are you trying to work through an issue or make someone else look bad?
>> Have I received from you several e-mails that contradict with each other and obscure your intent?
>> Have I received an e-mail from you that says one thing about me but know of another e-mail to another person that says quite different things?
>> Have you copied my boss or others on something that we should have handled on our own?
>> Can I trust you not to send blind copies of my e-mail or your response?

In terms of reliability, have you always lived up to the digital commitments you've made to me? For example, if you have routinely said that you'd get back to me in 30 minutes and it often takes at least four hours, I do not trust that you are always reliable. If you promise work products by the end of the day, it's up to you to meet that commitment or let me know that you need to revise the time the work will be complete.

As for competence, the question is: Do I believe that you really have the ability to successfully complete the work I need done? If I believe that you need help in completing the task, then I do not trust that you are totally competent (yet) in this area.

Whatever the situation, how you manage your digital communication can profoundly affect the level of trust in your business relationships. If our digital communications raise questions regarding sincerity (intent), reliability, and/or competence, then we have reduced others' trust in us. And because these injuries in trust happen suddenly, and may be difficult to spot because of subtle nuances, they can erode our relationships without our even realizing it.

Getting people to trust your organization is also critical. The Internet allows customers to speak to a company directly, and the way that company responds to their concerns will either create, deepen, or end relationships. The ability to hear, understand, and address concerns publicly—and quickly—is perhaps the best way to increase those customers' trust in your organization. Monitoring for and fixing problems proves that your business is actively listening, that you can take feedback/criticism about your product or service, and that your firm is committed to providing great customer service. The customer now has a voice, and it is the wise firm that facilitates such communication.

Key #4: Share Information to Increase Your Personal Power

Let's start with a life-or-death example of sharing to increase personal power. Countless people in the Arab Spring uprisings of 2012 found digitally sharing information to be central to increasing their personal power—and to saving their lives. Iranian dissidents use Twitter and Facebook as relationship-development tools in their country, which tries to censor free expression. It turns out that Twitter is very, very hard to censor. Jonathan Zittrain, a professor at Harvard Law School, explains this by saying:

> Twitter was particularly resilient to censorship because it had so many ways for its posts to originate—from a phone, a Web browser, or specialized applications—and so many outlets for those posts to appear. As each new home for this material

becomes a new target for censorship, a repressive system faces a game of whack-a-mole in blocking Internet address after Internet address carrying the subversive material. . . . It is easy for Twitter feeds to be echoed everywhere else in the world. The qualities that make Twitter seem inane and half-baked for example, [I'm now having eggs for breakfast.] are what makes it so powerful.[19]

Twitter and Facebook were also used by the countries elsewhere in the Arab Spring uprisings. In Egypt and Tunisia, for example, Twitter, Facebook, and blogging platforms allowed protesters to communicate with each other and with the outside world, showing police trying to suppress the democratic impulse. Here is what the Public Broadcasting System (PBS) had to say about social media in the Arab Spring beginning December 2010–2013:

> In the age of 21st century technology, social media is being credited for igniting the recent protests in Egypt, Tunisia, and other parts of the Arab world. For several years, online blogs and social media have been increasingly important tools used by activists in Egypt, a country with five million Facebook users.[20]

While these life-or-death examples come from political uprisings, we have seen how powerfully these same tools have been used for global and multinational projects. These digital tools allow Joan Holmes, founding president of The Hunger Project, to share information with many more people in her quest to end world hunger. As Holmes says:

> The world can now end hunger. . . . I'm really here to develop a partnership with you so that we can work together on this great human endeavor. . . . Everyone is the key. Because everyone has his or her own unique contribution to make to something this big. My job [is] to let them all know about the end of hunger and that they are key. I also need to facilitate them finding their contribution to make.

That was the partnership that I was interested in—that we would all stand shoulder to shoulder, looking at a shared vision and then working together to share our specific skills to achieve that vision.[21]

Would Holmes be able to mount this vision without digital communication's sharing power? Perhaps, but it would be even more challenging and take much more time. Knowing that key people are looking out for her e-mails allows Holmes to stay in touch in ways not possible 30 years ago.

Holmes' project focuses on world hunger, but it could just as easily be on a global business project, requiring close communication among 50 people in 25 nations. Those of us old enough to remember what used to happen when businesses tried to do such projects on conference calls will have no difficulty seeing the potential benefits of e-mail or other forms of digital communication. We can vividly recall 12 people interrupting each other, many staying silent, and the meeting leader repeatedly calling for order. For a modern and improved update of this meeting, consider Steve Jobs launching a new Apple product through teleconference to thousands of his employees, generating enthusiasm and understanding.

Facebook, the fastest-growing of all the online platforms, now with well over 1 billion users in 2013, also provides ways to increase your personal power. Facebook started as a way for college students to connect with fellow classmates on campus, first digitally and then in person. The platform then became more mainstream (first opening up to high school students and eventually to the general public); Facebook's focus from the very beginning was to connect individuals.

In 2007, Facebook introduced "Pages" to the platform—a way for brands, organizations, and celebrities to create their own presence and connect with the 300 million or so individuals already using the site. For the first time, the person-to-person relationship barrier was expanded, and business-to-customer (B2C) and business-to-business (B2B) marketing opportunities were introduced. Since then, brands have been evolving the way they interact with their "fans," and their critics. As with most other social media platforms, brands that treat this new environment with a personalized approach tend to be more successful. As an example of a firm that has gained power by sharing on Facebook, here is the story of the Got What It Cakes Facebook page:

> When Mandie Miller left her job as an on-air traffic reporter in Charlotte, North Carolina, to have her first child, she started baking cakes for friends, just for fun. The response was so positive that in April 2009, she started a business, Got What It Cakes. Ms Miller put up a Web site, but about five months later her sister created a Got What It Cakes Facebook page. This is when the business started to grow. Cake orders went from two or three a weekend to six to 10; now Ms Miller is turning away another 10 each weekend. Annual revenue at the end of her second year in business was a little more than $40,000.[22]

Without Facebook, it would have taken much longer for Ms. Miller to establish herself and her business. *In two years, Miller now has 5,000 fans on Facebook and spends a fair amount of time communicating with those fans, exchanging recipes, childcare tips, and kid stories.* Imagine how difficult it would be to establish this fan base face to face, in snail mail, or over the phone. And any number of businesses have sprung up to help businesses like hers set up an effective Facebook page—sharing their wares and increasing their personal and professional power.

Key #5: Manage Yourself Before You Manage Others

Last, we return to the drunken monkey—that internal chatter that can spark fear, defensiveness, and negativity. Earlier we said that a businessperson trying to be more effective must have a clear sense of what his shortcomings are so that he can recognize them before they scuttle business or personal relationships. If something in our digital communications has awakened our drunken monkey, we have learned that we need to stop and take a break before we fire back an e-mail or post a comment. Defensiveness limits our personal power. So managing ourselves before we communicate digitally becomes critical.

Twitter users are perhaps the poster children for "manage yourself before you manage others." Given the brevity of the communication and its instantaneousness, users need to be very clear about who they are before hitting SEND. If your tweets come across as weak, defensive, or angry, you can very quickly damage both your reputation and that of your firm. The same is true with blogs. Readers will accept ongoing tirades from bloggers, but only if there is a clear reason for the outcry.

On an individual basis, managing yourself effectively online means being aware of who you are and what you post. How would her 5,000 subscribers act if Mandie Miller, on her Cakes Facebook site, suddenly became petulant and petty? Those sharing information online must be increasingly cognizant of the types of information shared and the manner in which they are conducting themselves because those two things hold significant implications for potential future relationships. Just as sharing good information can increase personal power, sharing bad or inappropriate information can seriously limit that power. In a world where digital information is a keystroke away, online communicators can easily hurt themselves by sharing pictures of themselves drunk at a party (or worse).

On an organizational level, managing "yourself" primarily refers to staying on brand with your posts and comments, as well as staying sensible. In 2008, Ford Motor Company forgot about the sensible when it threatened legal action against members of the Black Mustang Club. As the Adrants blog reported:

> While brands certainly don't want people using their products, logos, and other related imagery to create products of their own,

the hammer that Ford legal dropped on the Black Mustang Club [was] ... heavy handed. Recently the club created a calendar which contained images of club members' cars photographed by the members themselves. Ford didn't take kindly to this and asked CafePress, the service the group had chosen to print the calendars, to kill the project, claiming [that] all the images in the calendar are the property of Ford ... including the Black Mustang Club logo. .... It's understandable that a brand would and should do everything it can to protect itself from any kind of potential negative effect, but to attack a group of people who, clearly, love the product in question simply for showing their love of that product is, well, idiotic and more harmful to the brand than had they done nothing at all.[23]

In a misguided attempt to protect its brand, Ford Motor Company's legal department came down hard on Mustang enthusiasts, customers who had been aggressively selling the Ford brand for years to other people. Luckily for Ford, cooler, nonlegal heads prevailed, and the club's calendar was okayed forever. Managing yourself is not simply about dealing with defensiveness; it can also help to protect us and our relationships when we are feeling most vulnerable.

Conclusion

As Tom Peters has said, "All dealings are personal dealings in the end."[24] Experience tells us that the more technologically focused society becomes, the more important relationships become. Paying attention to the five keys in our digital communication can increase the likelihood of developing powerful business relationships and can make our lives easier and more productive.

POINTS TO REMEMBER

» Every digital communication to customers that your employees send is a marketing communication. As you have a vice president of marketing who crafts the messages regarding your firm and its offerings, so you similarly need some sort of control on your digital messaging. A social media marketing manager can help you to minimize problems by coming up with guidelines about the sorts of messages that your firm does—and does not—send.

» Consider distributing lessons from Charles Newkey-Burden's book, *Great Email Disasters*, or David Shipley and Will Schwalbe's book, *Send: The Essential Guide to Email for Office and Home*. These books—better than any others we know—show the pitfalls of sending or answering an e-mail too quickly, with too little thought. And they are sometimes hilarious.

» Ask your employees to share effective digital messages or websites they come across. It's helpful to model the writing behaviors you are after.

» If you have already determined which of your employees are effective writers, use them to communicate with customers through your chosen online platforms.

For Leaders: Three Relationship Challenges

our ability as a leader to develop powerful relationships—both within your company and with those outside it—will be fundamental to your success. Although all the keys we've discussed thus far are important, you have three additional unique relationship challenges as a leader.

Three Unique Relationship Challenges for Leaders

As a business leader, you depend on relationships to get most of your work done and you face some unique relationship challenges. Although we could clearly write a book about the importance of relationships for business leaders and managers, that is not our purpose here. For now, we would just like to focus on three significant relationship challenges that we believe are critical to your success:

1. Staying true to yourself
2. Managing multiple types of relationships
3. Installing a culture that promotes powerful business relationships

Before we examine these three challenges, however, let's look at the special relationship that exists between you and those you lead.

The Relationship between You and Those You Lead

Your ability as a leader to create and develop powerful relationships has been and will be fundamental to your success. In part, this is so because the mantle of leadership is ultimately bestowed on you by others. That is, you are not a leader unless others allow you to lead them. John Kotter, in "What Leaders Really Do," argues that management and leadership are different but complementary. He defines the differences in the following graph that we created below[1]:

MANAGEMENT	LEADERSHIP
Focuses on coping with complexity and bringing order and consistency	Focuses on coping with change
Emphasizes: • Planning and budgeting • Organizing and staffing • Controlling and problem solving	Emphasizes: • Setting a direction, a vision of the future • Aligning people around a shared vision • Motivating and inspiring to keep people moving in the same direction

Looking at Kotter's distinctions in the right-hand column of our chart, you can see that leaders articulate visions, align people, and then motivate them to execute those visions. Thus the leader's world is about creating a direction and context for action; it is left to those who follow to translate the vision into reality. Because these responsibilities complement each other, leaders and followers often develop a special relationship that includes high levels of trust, confidence in, and commitment to the vision and priorities. When people you lead lose trust or confidence in you and your vision, your relationships become much more difficult and business results suffer. People begin to second-guess you, withhold support, and move more slowly, perhaps in different directions. At this point you may be called their "leader," but you exist as a leader in name only. It's important to note here that leaders are not necessarily leaders simply because of their "positional power." Most successful leaders we know depend more on their "personal power"—generated as a result of strong relationships—to attain extraordinary business results.

Your Relationships Have Gotten You Where You Are

Some of those who first recognized you as a potential business leader were your bosses, mentors, and colleagues. As we mentioned earlier, although technical skills may have helped certain people early in their careers, it has been their ability to develop strong business relationships that has enabled them to emerge as leaders.

Having had strong relationships with those in high places, though, was not all that got you to your current job. Along the way, you have also had to demonstrate your ability to develop strong relationships internally, with colleagues and direct reports, and externally, with customers and other business partners. Ultimately, you demonstrated that you could influence and motivate others to commit to your vision and travel with you along often uncharted paths.

Challenge #1: Staying True to Yourself

We spoke about the importance of managing yourself as one key to develop powerful business relationships. A critical element in self-management is staying true to yourself. While this can be a challenge for some of us, it can be a particularly challenging task for a leader. Jack Welch is quoted as saying that one of the best pieces of advice he ever got was from Paul Austin, former chairman of Coca-Cola, early in his executive career. Observing Welch being very quiet in a General Electric board meeting, Austin said to Welch, "Jack, don't forget who you are and how you got here." And, as Welch says, the "next meeting, I think I spoke up a bit."[2] Austin's prompting allowed Welch to realize that, as a new board member, he had suddenly begun behaving differently and needed to reclaim himself. This uncharacteristic behavior does not surprise us.

Many of the senior leaders we know who have been promoted into senior leadership roles will privately concede that they were initially at a loss as to how to add value in their new roles. Having inherited or chosen talented direct reports who were particularly adept at handling the technical aspects of the business, we have heard new senior managers privately wondering: What is left for me to do? Yet, while these new leaders were just getting their feet wet, their direct reports were expecting them to lead and make significant decisions almost immediately. With these raised expectations and an expanded scope of responsibility, many new leaders admitted that it was challenging to stay true to themselves, especially with things coming at them so fast. They hadn't yet had time to think about an issue, and certainly didn't know what was best to do. As a result, those without a strong moral compass to provide clarity within the ambiguity that comes with change, fell back to managing tasks, not relationships. But those who were able to stay true to themselves and manage their initial anxiety began to listen more and seek feedback. That, in turn, allowed them to increase trust, develop powerful relationships, and find the best business solutions.

The transition from manager to leader is often not an easy one. Despite sometimes having documented job descriptions and/or clear mandates from bosses or boards, this transition can be a profound shift. It requires you to move from the tactical to the strategic and from managing a process to motivating and aligning people around a vision and strategy. This transition requires new leaders *to see themselves differently.* Nowhere is this more evident than in the transition from president to CEO. Because the role of the CEO can seem so amorphous, the transition is often disorienting. These former presidents, who are used to being in control and accustomed to having all their bases covered, find themselves facing higher expectations, increasing ambiguity and higher levels of accountability from many sources in the midst of this transition. It is easy at this point for leaders to lose themselves and compromise their values amidst the urgency to perform. To prevent this, some executive coaches suggest that future leaders, long before they attain executive status, write what they believe in with regard to people to ensure that they gain clarity about what is important to them. Those coaches believe that by documenting their values, these individuals will have a reliable compass later on that keeps them centered and authentic—or true to themselves.

Randy Komisar, ex-CEO of LucasArts, the former American video game licensor, describes the challenge of maintaining authenticity as a manager moves into leadership:

> We begin life on a linear path where success is based on having a clear target. Life gets complicated when the targets aren't clear anymore and you have to set your own targets. By rubbing up against the world, you get to know yourself. Either do that or you're going to spend your life serving the interests and expectations of others.[3]

One excellent example of a leader who started with established values and developed from there is Howard Schultz, ex-CEO of Starbucks Coffee. Some of Schultz's values had been formed by an early crisis. When he was seven years old, in 1961, his father broke his ankle on the ice and lost his delivery job. There was no workers' compensation and no unemployment, and the Schultz family struggled because the father's job offered no health insurance. Let Bill George, the very successful CEO of Medtronics, take up the story:

> Schultz vowed [that] he would do it differently when he had the opportunity. He dreamed of building a company that treated its employees well and provided health care benefits. Little did he realize that one day he would be responsible for 140,000 employees working in 11,000 Starbucks stores worldwide.... Memories of his father's lack of health care led Schultz to make Starbucks the first American company to provide access to health care for qualified employees who work as few as twenty hours per week.[4]

In a 2007 article in the *Harvard Business Review*, Bill George and colleagues reach a conclusion on what it takes to be an effective leader. After interviewing several hundred leaders in their research, George concludes by saying:

> [W]e believe [that] we understand why more than 1,000 studies have not produced a profile of an ideal leader. Analyzing 3,000 pages of transcripts, our team was startled to see that these people did not identify any universal characteristics, traits, skills, or styles that led to their success. *Rather, their leadership emerged from their life stories.* Consciously and subconsciously, they were constantly testing themselves through real-world experiences and reframing their life stories to understand who they were at their core. In doing so, they discovered the purpose of their leadership and learned that being authentic made them more effective[5] [italics added].

Another way to approach authentic leadership—being true to oneself—comes from Harry M. Jansen Kraemer, Jr., who wrote the book, *From Values to Action: The Four Principles of Values-Based Leadership.* In an excerpted section of the book that appeared on Forbes.com, Kraemer says that there are four rules of authentic leadership: (1) self-reflection—the ability to identify and reflect on what you stand for, what your values are, and what matters most to you; (2) balance—the ability to see situations from multiple perspectives and differing viewpoints to gain a much fuller understanding; (3) true self-confidence—accepting yourself as you are; and (4) genuine humility—never forget who you are or where you came from.

Using these rules, Kraemer moved from being a junior analyst at Baxter Healthcare to becoming the chairman and CEO of the multi-billion-dollar-health-care company. Then he used the four principles to align with his values so as to serve effectively as a CEO and as a professor at Kellogg Business School; as an executive partner with Madison Dearborn Partners, a Chicago-based private equity firm with a portfolio of more than 40 companies; and as a member of about a dozen boards of for-profit and not-for-profit organizations.[6]

Finally, perhaps the greatest difficulty in staying true to self for senior leaders lies in maintaining their growing web of relationships. The more successful they become, the easier it is for them to forget where they came from and who helped them get where they are now. It's easy to lose perspective.

For others, the need for greater power and wealth can become addictive. They are never satisfied. They have to get the next big deal, the next million, or the next prize—whatever the cost. Add to that Wall Street's demand for increasing short-term profits and the leader's escalating fear of failure, and you have some major causes for executives losing their way—and themselves. You could argue that Gordon Gekko, in the movie *Wall Street*, is authentic, but he exists only for himself and for profit. Gekko fosters relationships only to allow himself to get what he wants. In the movie *Arbitrage*, Richard Gere's character is so focused on financial success and getting the next big deal—ostensibly for his family's security—that he loses the love and respect of the family members he is trying to protect. The quest for gaining more and more power and acquiring greater and greater wealth can become an all-consuming slippery slope. This slope begins when business leaders, who have prospered beyond their wildest dreams, can never get enough money, recognition, or power. We have asked them, "How much is enough?" and "When will you feel secure?" Depending on their level of self-awareness, they may quietly admit that there will probably never be enough money or power to satisfy them. Those can be the saddest conversations of all because such executives may have lost a healthy relationship with themselves and, most probably, with many others. They may be truly alone.

Challenge #2: Managing Multiple Relationships

As you assume positions of greater influence and authority, more and more people want your time and attention. Depending on your position, you may need to handle a wide range of constituencies from direct reports to customers, suppliers, boards of directors, financial analysts, industry associations, government entities, and the press. Jerry MacArthur Hultin, senior presidential fellow of New York University, former president of the Polytechnic Institute of New York University, and former undersecretary of the US Navy, focused the business schools he ran on innovation and economic growth. In a personal interview Hultin talks about the demands placed on him as a leader and the tools he has developed to manage all those relationships:

> An organization or person that is transforming or growing or hungry to change tends to need a lot more contact with new opportunities. But after decades of networking, I've got way too many relationships to manage. . . . there must be over 7,000 names in my iPad and iPhone. You can't relate to 7,000 people, even sixty minutes a year per contact consumes every waking hour of your life. So if I am not careful, I'd be drowning in contacts and my relationships will go nowhere. So to manage this, I move many people up or down on my relationship-investment scale. It's a matter of triage.
>
> If you are really good at collecting initial relationships, you need to be part of an organization that allows you to hand off your contacts to others. You need to be part of an organization that values new relationships and knows how to build their own connection with the people I meet. I probably exchange a hundred business cards a week, so that means I have 100 people who want to be in a relationship with me. I can't possibly sustain these relationships, so I have a system for distributing these people and their cards to the most appropriate person on my staff—my research provost, or career development director, or admissions officer. I use a form I've developed and notes that I have made so that my colleagues can follow up and build a meaningful relationship with many of the people I meet.
>
> At some point, though, I do think you reach a saturation point. If you are in an organization which is doing well, your challenge isn't so much "mining" all the people you meet; rather, it is culling

down your relationships to the 10 out of 100 or 1 out of 100 that really have value. The problem is that when first meeting someone, during the first two or three meetings, you really don't know what will become of the relationship. So you have an early dilemma: how much time should I invest to find out whether there is, from a business side or a collaborative side, something worth pursuing?

Of course, over time, a relationship may take on a new, different value. For example, a business relationship may turn into a personal friendship, but in the beginning you just don't know. My style has been to have more relationships than I truly need because I understand that many relationships are likely to evolve over time. What may be a fairly moderate relationship initially may become very rich when a new project comes up, when there is a new direction in your firm, or when the market shifts.

For example, just today I was talking to a major American corporation that is seeking a new market in China, especially in urban areas. I'm sure they will do a lot of business in China's cities. As I laid out what we are doing in China, they were impressed with one organization that is very influential in setting policy and training leaders in China. It took me nearly 10 years to build a relationship with this Chinese organization. And when I started to build this relationship in 2003, it was not clear what would grow from knowing this organization. Now, with NYU's and China's greater and greater focus on the cities yet to be built, the relationship has become quite valuable.

If you looked at my calendar in 2003, you would see at least twenty other, equally interesting relationships in which I was investing some time. It turns out that I've done less with some of these relationships, even though at the time, some seemed likely to be valuable and productive.

That's why I think that it is important to have a broad range of relationships. Some people develop relationships in other ways. For instance, some people are very precise and only focus on relationships with others that offer high returns in the coming three months. I've taken a broader view.

Every time something good happens, many people say it was luck. Of course, this trivializes the power and richness of relationships. To me, "luck" is what a rich set of relationships produces. It's not that you are lucky; it's that you created an environment in which things that others call "lucky" happen.

It's not luck, it's actually the result of the way one builds value. ***Without relationships, you may be brilliant, but its unlikely that the world will get the benefit of your brilliance.*** If a person is good or smart or capable at something and, secondly, if the person has a strong network of relationships, the person's skills are likely to be appreciated and applied to opportunities of consequence.[7]

To put this in a slightly different way, an effective leader needs to be a juggler of relationships, deciding which to invest in, how much to invest, and when to invest.

Challenge #3: Installing a Culture that Promotes Healthy, Empowering Relationships

Your third unique challenge as a leader is to create the context in which powerful business relationships can grow and thrive. This requires that you pay particular attention to culture and alignment. When aligned around common vision and goals within an aligned structure, you have leveraged the power of your people. When structure and culture are not aligned, your organization struggles, failing to fully execute your strategy or realize your vision. Often this leads to dysfunction, a toxic environment where work is at the very least unpleasant and results disappointing. A major part of your job is to promote a healthy culture in which people, teams, and organizations can succeed by working together productively. You are ultimately responsible for the health of your organization.

So how do you begin to develop a healthy culture? Often new leaders first look at changing the way the team and/or business is structured, believing that by merely changing reporting structures, most problems will be solved. Although reorganizing is something a new leader can do to symbolically signal change, new leaders can actually reduce alignment by changing the reporting structures without a clear vision or goals, and without thinking about possible unintended consequences.

Now, don't get us wrong. We believe in changing structure to realign a team or organization. For us, though, the question is: What is the context within which you are restructuring? Without a clear vision, goals, and strategy, several differing structures might work. Where are you leading the organization? If you don't know, any road will take you there, and different organizational structures may work. Because organizational structure has such a profound impact on how your company works, the rationale for structural change needs to be carefully considered. There is no perfect structure. Usually, the best you can hope for is creating a structure aligned with your vision that empowers powerful relationships, all working toward a common goal. As goals change, structures may also need to change again, but without a common goal and an aligned structure, it is tough—if not impossible—to work as a team.

Although new leaders may be more comfortable changing organizational structure, creating a healthy culture is a far more daunting task. Leaders "own" their culture. No one else in the organization has greater impact on culture than you, the leader. So it is important that you understand what you are getting into when you start thinking about culture.

What Is Culture Anyway?

It is those beliefs, values, and norms (written and unwritten rules) that guide behavior. They help people to answer such questions as: How open and honest can I be? How much information should I share? How do decisions get made? How much tolerance does this organization have for risk taking? How does this organization usually handle disagreement and conflict? Is leadership shared or closely held?

If people work within the beliefs, values, and norms, then they will succeed and get promoted; when people violate those norms, either intentionally or unintentionally, they will struggle in their jobs and possibly fail. This sounds simple enough, but it isn't. Remember that there are unwritten rules, too. You know—or should know—the policies and procedures that have been documented in the "official" company handbook. Although these, too, can be problematic at times and might require updating, the norms or unwritten rules are more powerful and more difficult to discover and manage. Some have found that certain corporate norms are so powerful that they are not safe to discuss.

The unwritten rules generally are the way things *really* work. These come from what people see others do that either gets them ahead or in trouble. If we joined your company and wanted to figure out how things really worked, this is what we would do: (1) we would read the official policy manual, and (2) after several weeks, one of us would find someone in your company (you) who seems to be well respected, trustworthy, and approachable. We would invite you for a drink some day after work to find out how things *really work* at the company. That way we could avoid saying or doing things that would get us in trouble, and we would learn what we need to do to fit in.

This conversation begins to reveal some of the unwritten rules of your company. For example, you may tell us that no matter what the manual says about being on time to work, the truth is that no one really notices what time you get in unless you are more than 30 minutes late. In fact, managers generally don't come in until 9 a.m., a full hour after the posted start time. Or you might say that although our boss encourages everyone to feel free to disagree with him, the last person who told the boss what she really thought was then characterized as a trouble-maker. Now her career is pretty much on hold. By now we are beginning to get the picture of how to be successful in your company.

As a leader, you need to remember that unwritten rules ***arise not from what you say, but from what people see (or believe they see) you or other leaders doing.*** If you say you want a culture that promotes collaboration but constantly reward those who are only out for themselves, people will soon learn that the unwritten rule is: The heck with everyone else; win at all costs. If you say, "Value everyone's opinion" but only listen to a trusted few, people will learn that the unwritten rule is: Only a few people's opinions really count. Thankfully, not all unwritten rules are counterproductive. Some unwritten rules actually support work by allowing the team to take shortcuts or support one another. The challenge for you as a leader is to begin to discover what the unwritten rules might be, which unwritten rules are productive, and which are counterproductive and need to be addressed. To uncover these unwritten rules, though, the team must trust that it is safe for them to tell you the truth. That is a tall order. Unless they tell the truth or you have someone from outside your organization create that space for you, you will have an extremely difficult time creating norms that drive a healthy, performance-based culture.

Finally, and we are repeating ourselves here, remember that when it comes to culture, what you as a leader say—and, *more important, what you do*—really matters! You will choose to promote healthy business relationships or not. That choice, we submit, will make a big difference in your team performance.

Dee Hock, who founded and grew Visa into a multi-billion-dollar company, is one example of someone who uses values to drive a corporate culture. He started by meditating on the nature of community, and finally decided that it was based on a "non-monetary exchange of value." What is exchanged in community is the "soft stuff"—care, respect, tolerance, generosity, and acting for the good of the place. Because it's nonmonetary, it cannot be measured, as we have seen earlier. This makes the exchange difficult for those who rely on quantification and measurement. In our paraphrase, he talks about how the self and community values are interconnected:

In a true community, unity of the "singular one" and the "plural one" applies as well to beliefs, purpose, and principles. Some we hold in common with all others in the community. Some we hold in common with only part of the community. Others we may hold alone. In true community, we respect and tolerate the values others hold, even if we do not share them—either because we realize that our beliefs will require respect and tolerance in return, or because we know those who hold different beliefs will understand and respect the common humanity that transcends all difference.

True community also requires proximity—continual interaction between the people, places, and things of which it is composed. Throughout history, the basic community, the fundamental social building block, has always been the family. It is there that the greatest nonmonetary exchange of value takes place. It is there that the most powerful nonmaterial values are created and exchanged. It is from the community called family, for better or worse, that all other communities are formed.

Without any one of the three nonmaterial values—tolerance, nonmonetary exchange of value, and proximity—no true community ever existed or ever will. If we were to set out to design an efficient system for the methodical destruction of community, we could do no better than our present efforts to monetize all value and reduce life to the tyranny of measurement. Money, markets, and measurement have their place. They are important tools indeed. We should honor and use them. But they do not deserve the deification their apostles demand of us, before which we too readily sink to our knees. *Only fools worship their tools.*[8]

Is there any way to determine the financial results that culture drives? In his book, *The Culture Cycle: How to Shape the Unseen Force that Transforms Performance*, James Heskett studied dozens of high-performing firms and concluded:

[A]s much as half the difference in operating profit between organizations can be attributed to effective cultures. In addition, an

organization's culture provides significant competitive advantage in bad times, such as those we've seen in recent years. All of this is possible with little or no capital investment, yielding an infinite ROI [return on investment]. All it requires is the time of leaders.[9]

Heskett interviewed Herb Kelleher, founder of Southwest Airlines, and asked

... how he and his fellow founders had thought about mission, values, and strategy at the beginning [1969]. His response was as follows: At the beginning, we said, "stop wasting time on five- or ten-year plans. We want to start an airline. Culture comes first; what we're about is protecting and growing people. The questions we asked were "What do we want to be? What do we want to do for the world? ... We wanted to be the airline for the common man.[10]

It's very hard to argue with Southwest's bottom line.

Conclusion: Changing Cultures

In the preceding section we have been talking about your impact as a leader when creating and aligning a corporate culture. Building a healthy culture from the ground up is one thing, but changing a culture is yet another—and definitely not for the faint of heart. Cultural change is a "wicked" problem. Unlike most "tame" problems[11]—those with clear beginnings and endings—cultural change is ongoing. It requires working in the middle, where things can be complicated, ambiguous, and chaotic. Once you think the problem has been solved, something happens to suggest, given the circumstance, that there may be a better way to solve it. Cultural change requires leaders and managers to have the mental space to hold complex priorities and views without becoming overwhelmed. A well-thought-out, integrated team approach that engages people while building and reinforcing momentum can go a long way toward making the cultural change process productive and rewarding—but this is clearly a journey, not a project.

POINTS TO REMEMBER

» Stay true to yourself. Get clear about your values and your vision so that you can authentically communicate them to others. Write down your most important values.

» Find a tool or a process to manage an increasing number of multiple types of business relationships. Decide
  ○ Which relationships are your priorities?
  ○ Which can be managed by others?

» Take a look at your team's or organization's culture. Does it promote powerful business relationships so that it unleashes the power of your organization? If it does not, what must you do to fix it?

Transform your business relationships into powerful ones. Build more productive and effective individual, team, and other critical B2B relationships. Visit FiveKeysBook.com for additional tools and resources.

Annotated Bibliography

Relationship Before Task

Cohen, Allan R., and David L. Bradford. *Influence without Authority.*
New York: Wiley, 1989 and 1991.

> A cornerstone book. The worker/manager of tomorrow will need
> to be able to get things done through teams outside the bounds
> of his or her formal authority. This means that such workers/
> managers will have to know well both themselves and those
> whom they will be trying to influence. This book contains one
> of the most useful explications of the social exchange theory
> that we have seen. The chart on page 79 entitled, "Currencies
> Frequently Valued in Organizations," may be worth the price of
> the book for those struggling with what motivates people. We
> think that this book will be especially helpful for those in leader-
> ship positions.

Trust

Covey, Stephen M. R. *The Speed of Trust: The One Thing that Changes
Everything.* New York: Free Press, 2006.

> As Covey says, "I contend that the ability to establish, grow,
> extend, and restore trust is not only vital to our personal and
> interpersonal well-being; it is *the* key leadership competency

of the new global economy" (p. 2). We agree. What is special about this book is that Covey, in example after example, shows the dollar value coming from speed based on trust. At the same time, he offers practical ways to speed up the development of trust that every businessperson should know about. A book well worth your time.

Self-knowledge

George, Bill, and Peter Sims. *True North: Discover Your Authentic Leadership.* San Francisco: Jossey-Bass, 2007.

Bill George is the wildly successful ex-CEO of Medtronics who believes that you have to know who you are and what you believe before you can lead others. As he says, "Without being aware of your vulnerabilities, fears, and longings, it is hard to empathize with others who are experiencing similar feelings" (p. 71). During the research for this book, he and his team spoke to 125 other CEOs of major companies. The interviews show that those CEOs, too, gained self-knowledge and put principle before profit but ended up making more profit than they believe they would have otherwise. Listen to the CEOs of many Fortune 100 firms tell their stories, and see how they view relationship skills as a critical business skill that produces hard-dollar results.

Relationship before Task

Gittell, Jody Hoffer. *The Southwest Airlines Way: Using the Power of Relationships to Achieve High Performance.* New York, McGraw-Hill, 2003.

This a fascinating case study of what happens when a firm starts out knowing that relationships are the key to productivity and uses them as the basis for designing its culture. The book is filled with examples of Southwest making choices that are 180 degrees away from traditional business practices, and yet Southwest remains the most profitable carrier in a shrinking industry. The book is easy to read and a great testament to hiring people based on their "relational competence."

For Leaders

Hock, Dee. *One from Many: VISA and the Rise of the Chaordic Organization.* San Francisco: Barrett-Koehler, 2005.

> How often will you get a CEO who has built a multi-billion-dollar company to sit down with you and explain exactly how he did it? Unlikely at best. But that is what Dee Hock does in this book. You see him face all three of the leadership challenges we present and many more—getting bankers to agree with each other, working with competitors, and developing a culture that empowered people to be the best they can.

Relationship before Task

Kuzmeski, Maribeth. *The Connectors: How the World's Most Successful Businesspeople Build Relationships and Win Clients for Life.* Hoboken, NJ: Wiley, 2009.

> This book concentrates on how effective salespeople develop and maintain relationships. What's particularly nice is its focus on specific skills such as listening and the self-assessments and checklists scattered throughout. It's one of those books where the best salespeople will already know most of the points that Kuzmeski describes, but they will read it because they are the best salespeople—there will be behaviors they need to sharpen or a few skills they need to develop.

Self-knowledge

Mintzberg, Henry. *Managers Not MBAs: A Hard Look at the Soft Practice of Managing and Management Development.* San Francisco: Barrett-Koehler, 2004–2005.

> We are big fans of Mintzberg not only because he does an excellent job at describing the human complexities of management but also because he cared enough to create the International Management Program in Practicing Management (IMPM). The IMPM is a graduate business school that starts with self-reflection and works at human issues *and* analytical processes.

The book gives you the opportunity to rethink some of your hiring criteria for managers and to develop some very useful approaches to teams and problem solving.

Self-knowledge

Bradberry, Travis, and Jean Greaves. *Emotional Intelligence 2.0.* New York: TalentSmart, 2009.

Based on Daniel Goleman's great *Emotional Intelligence: Why It Can Matter more than IQ, 10th Anniversary Edition* (New York, Bantam Press, 2006), this book breaks down self-knowledge into dozens of specific behaviors so that you can work on understanding people more effectively and, in the process, be much more productive. The book includes a link so that you can self-test your own emotional intelligence to establish a baseline against which you can measure your improvements.

Bibliography

Argyris, Chris. "Teaching Smart People How to Learn." *Harvard Business Review*, June 1991.

Autry, James A. *Love and Profit: The Art of Caring Leadership*. New York: Avon Books, 1992.

Ayers, Alex, ed. *The Wit and Wisdom of Mark Twain*. New York: Harper Perennial, 2005.

Beckman, Howard B., Kathryn M. Markakis, Anthony L. Suchman, and Richard M. Frankel. "The Doctor-Patient Relationship and Malpractice: Lessons from Plaintiff Depositions." *JAMA Internal Medicine* 154(12), June 1994.

Boorstin, Julia. "The Best Advice I Ever Got: Warren Buffett, Richard Branson, Meg Whitman, A. G. Lafley, and 24 Other Luminaries on the People Who Most Influenced Their Lives." *Fortune*, March 21, 2005.

Chafkin, Max. "The Zappos Way of Managing." *Inc.*, May 1, 2009.

Cohen, Allan R., and David L. Bradford. *Influence without Authority*. New York: Wiley, 1991.

Covey, Stephen M. R. *The Speed of Trust: The One Thing that Changes Everything*. New York: Free Press, 2006.

Deming, W. Edwards. *Out of the Crisis*. Cambridge, MA: MIT Press, 1986.

Freeman, Douglas Southall. *Lee's Lieutenants: A Study in Command; Cedar Mountain to Chancellorsville*, Vol. 2. New York: Scribner, 1943.

Friedman, Thomas L. *The World Is Flat: A Brief History of the Twenty-First Century*. New York: Farrar, Straus & Giroux, 2005.

George, Bill. *True North: Discover Your Authentic Leadership*. San Francisco: Jossey-Bass, 2007.

George, Bill. "Leadership Starts with Self-Awareness." *Minneapolis Star Tribune*, February 26, 2012.

Gittell, Jody Hoffer. *The Southwest Airlines Way: Using the Power of Relationships to Achieve High Performance*. New York: McGraw-Hill, 2003.

Goleman, Daniel. "Flame First, Think Later: New Clues to Email Misbehavior." *New York Times*, February 20, 2007.

Goleman, Daniel. *Social Intelligence: The Revolutionary New Science of Human Relationships*. New York: Bantam Dell, 2007.

Goleman, Daniel. *Working with Emotional Intelligence*. New York: Bantam Books, 1998.

Hamel, Gary, and C. K. Prahalad. *Competing for the Future: Breakthrough Strategies for Seizing Control of Your Industry and Creating the Markets of Tomorrow*. Boston: Harvard Business School Press, 1994.

Hanson, Daniel S. *Cultivating Common Ground: Releasing the Power of Relationships at Work*. Woburn, MA: Butterworth-Heinemann, 1997.

Heskett, James. *The Culture Cycle: How to Shape the Unseen Force that Transforms Performance*. Upper Saddle River, NJ: Financial Times Press, 2012.

Hock, Dee. *One from Many: VISA and the Rise of Chaordic Organization*. San Francisco: Barrett-Koehler, 2005.

Isaacson, Walter. *Benjamin Franklin: An American Life*. New York: Simon & Schuster, 2003.

Kanter, Rosabeth Moss. *When Giants Learn to Dance: Mastering the Challenges of Strategy, Management, and Careers in the 1990s*. New York: Simon & Schuster, 1989.

Kern, Thomas, and Leslie P. Willcocks. *The Relationship Advantage: Information Technologies, Sourcing, and Management*. New York: Oxford University Press, 2001.

Kotter, John P. "What Leaders Really Do." *Harvard Business Review*, December 2001.

Kotter, John P., and James L. Heskett. *Corporate Culture and Performance*. New York: Free Press, 2011.

Kuzmeski, Maribeth. *The Connectors: How the World's Most Successful Businesspeople Build Relationships and Win Clients for Life*. Hoboken, NJ: Wiley, 2009.

Lee, Harper. *To Kill a Mockingbird*, 50th anniversary ed. New York: HarperCollins, 2011.

Maister, David H., Charles H. Green, and Robert M. Galford. *The Trusted Advisor*. New York: Free Press, 2000.

Mintzberg, Henry. *Managers Not MBAs: A Hard Look at the Soft Practice of Managing and Management Development.* San Francisco: Barrett-Koehler, 2005.

Newkey-Burden, Charles. *Great Email Disasters.* London: Metro Publishing, 2007.

O'Toole, James, and Warren Bennis. "What's Needed Next: A Culture of Candor." *Harvard Business Review,* June 2009.

Peters, Tom. *Liberation Management: Necessary Disorganization for the Nanosecond Nineties.* New York: Knopf, 1992.

Pink, Daniel H. *A Whole New Mind: Moving from the Information Age to the Conceptual Age.* New York: Riverhead Books, 2005.

Pirson, Michael, and Deepak Malhotra. "Unconventional Insights for Managing Stakeholder Trust." *Sloan Management Review,* July 1, 2008.

Rouse, Peter E. *Every Relationship Matters: Using the Power of Relationships to Transform Your Business, Your Firm, and Yourself.* Chicago: American Bar Association, 2007.

Shipley, David, and Will Schwalbe. *Send: The Essential Guide to Email for Office and Home.* New York: Knopf, 2007.

Tapscott, Don, and Anthony D. Williams. *Wikinomics: How Mass Collaboration Changes Everything,* expanded ed. New York: Portfolio, 2008.

Thurber, James. *Lanterns and Lances.* New York: Harper & Brothers, 1961.

Wheatley, Margaret J. *Leadership and the New Science: Learning about Organization from an Orderly Universe.* San Francisco: Barrett-Koehler, 1994.

Zeithaml, Valerie A., A. Parasuraman, and Leonard L. Berry. *Delivering Quality Service: Balancing Customer Perceptions and Expectations.* New York: Free Press, 1990.

Notes

Introduction and Overview of the Five Keys

1. Jody Hoffer Gittell, *The Southwest Airlines Way: Using the Power of Relationships to Achieve High Performance* (New York: McGraw-Hill, 2003), p. 85.

Why Care about Powerful Business Relationships?

1. Margaret J. Wheatley, *Leadership and the New Science: Learning about Organization from an Orderly Universe* (San Francisco: Barrett-Koehler, 1994), pp. 38–39.
2. Howard B. Beckman, Kathryn M. Markakis, Anthony L. Suchman, and Richard M. Frankel, "The Doctor-Patient Relationship and Malpractice: Lessons from Plaintiff Depositions," *JAMA Internal Medicine* 154(12):1365–1370, 1994. (We paraphrased in this section.)
3. W. Edwards Deming, *Out of the Crisis* (Cambridge, MA: MIT Press, 1986), p. 121.
4. *Ibid.*, p. 121.
5. *Ibid.*, pp. 121–222.
6. *Ibid.*, p. 123.
7. Daniel H. Pink, *A Whole New Mind: Moving from the Information Age to the Conceptual Age* (New York: Riverhead Books, 2005), pp. 1–2.
8. Jerry MacArthur Hultin, personal interview, November 2011.
9. Tom Peters, *Liberation Management: Necessary Disorganization for the Nanosecond Nineties* (New York: Alfred A. Knopf, 1992), p. 722.
10. Art van Bodegraven, personal interview, October 2011.

11. John P. Kotter and James L. Heskett, *Corporate Culture and Performance* (New York: Free Press, 2011), p. 11.

12. James Thomas, personal interview, June 2012.

13. Murray Bryant and Trevor Hunter, "BP and Public Issues (Mis) Management," *Ivey Business Journal*, September–October 2010, p. 1; available at: www.iveybusinessjournal.com/topics/leadership/bp-and -public-issues-mismanagement.

14. James A. Baker, III et al., "The Report of the BP U.S. Refineries Independent Safety Review Panel" ("The Baker Report"), BP, London; available at: www.bp.com/liveassets/bp_internet/globalbp/globalbp_ uk_english/SP/STAGING/local_assets/assets/pdfs/Baker _panel_report.pdf.

15. Murray Bryant and Trevor Hunter, "BP and Public Issues (Mis) Management," *Ivey Business Journal*, September–October 2010, p. 1; available at: www.iveybusinessjournal.com/topics/leadership/bp-and -public-issues-mismanagement.

16. Peter E. Rouse, *Every Relationship Matters: Using the Power of Relationships to Transform Your Business, Your Firm, and Yourself* (Chicago: American Bar Association, 2007), p. 56.

17. James Thomas, personal interview, September 2012.

18. Christine Birkner, "10 Minutes with . . . John Goodman," American Marketing Association, Alexandria, VA; available at: www .marketingpower.com/ResourceLibrary/Publications/Marketing News/2011/10-30-11/10-30-11 percent20pdfs/10 percent20 minutes.pdf.

19. Jody Hoffer Gittell, *The Southwest Airlines Way: Using the Power of Relationships to Achieve High Performance* (New York: McGraw-Hill, 2003), p. 85.

20. *Ibid.*, p. 7.

21. *Ibid.*, p. 125.

22. *Ibid.*, pp. 25–26.

23. Allan R. Cohen and David L. Bradford, *Influence Without Authority* (New York: Wiley, 1991), p. 79. (We paraphrased in this section.)

24. Rosabeth Moss Kanter, *When Giants Learn to Dance: Mastering the Challenges of Strategy, Management, and Careers in the 1990s* (New York: Simon & Schuster, 1989), p. 361.

25. Derek Smith, personal interview, June 2012.

26. Walter Isaacson, *Benjamin Franklin: An American Life* (New York: Simon & Schuster, 2003). p. 313.

Key #1: Connect First; Then Focus on Task

1. Daniel Goleman, *Social Intelligence: The Revolutionary New Science of Human Relationships* (New York: Bantam Dell, 2007), p. 4.
2. Jim Hallett, personal interview, September 2011.
3. *Ibid.*
4. *Ibid.*
5. *Ibid.*
6. *Ibid.*
7. Peter Goldsmith, personal interview, December 2011.
8. Paula Marshall, personal interview, January 2012.
9. Doug Renfro, personal interview, September 2011.
10. Tom Feeney, personal interview, September 2011.
11. Daniel S. Hanson, *Cultivating Common Ground: Releasing the Power of Relationships at Work* (Woburn, MA: Butterworth-Heinemann, 1997), pp. 62–63.
12. Bruce Barnes, personal interview, October 2011.
13. David H. Maister, Charles H. Green, and Robert M. Galford, *The Trusted Advisor* (New York: Free Press, 2000), p. 7.
14. Chris Vaughn, "Having Real Conversations with Consumers Will Drive Sales," Digital Sherpa, www.digitalsherpa.com/having-real-conversations-with-customers-will-drive-sales. (We paraphrased in this section.)
15. Matt Mickiewicz, "How Zappos Does Customer Service and Company Culture," SitePoint, www.sitepoint.com/how-zappos-does-customer-service-and-company-culture.
16. Max Chafkin, "The Zappos Way of Managing," *Inc.*, May 1, 2009, p. 12. (We paraphrased in this section.)

Key #2: Learn by Walking in Another's Shoes

1. Jack Fish, personal interview, September 2011.
2. Harper Lee, *To Kill a Mockingbird*, 50th anniversary edition (New York: HarperCollins, 2011), p. 48.
3. Dev Patnaik, "Innovation Starts with Empathy," Jump Associates, www.jumpassociates.com/innovation-starts-with-empathy.html. (We paraphrased in this section.)
4. Eve Tahmincioglu, "Empathy Can Go a Long Way at the Office," MSNBC, June 22, 2009; available at: www.primaryfreight.com/ads/PFpercent20MSNBCpercent206.22.09.pdf. (We paraphrased in this section.)

5. Nicholas Wolfson, personal interview, November 2011.
6. *Ibid.*
7. Joan Holmes, personal interview, October 2011.
8. Peter Goldsmith, personal interview, November 2011.
9. Nicholas Wolfson, personal interview, November 2011.
10. Joan Holmes, personal interview, October 2011.
11. Glen Stansberry, "10 Business Leaders You Should Strive to Emulate," Open Forum, February 25, 2010; available at: www.businessinsider .com/10-examples-of-excellent-business-leadership-2010-2?op=1. (We paraphrased in this section.)
12. Bruce Barnes, personal interview, October 2011.
13. Jim Hallett, personal interview, September 2011.
14. Jeff Schwantz, personal interview, October 2011.
15. Tom Feeney, personal interview, September 2011.
16. Thomas Kern and Leslie P. Willcocks, *The Relationship Advantage: Information Technologies, Sourcing, and Management* (New York: Oxford University Press, 2001), p. 217.
17. *Ibid.*, p. 258. (We paraphrased in this section.)

Key #3: Whether People Trust You Is Often up to You

1. Bruce Barnes, personal interview, October 2011.
2. In the 1950s, J. Thibaut, H. Kelley, and George Homans were some of the first to suggest that social behavior is based on an exchange. In the 1970s and 1980s, K. Cook and R. Emerson developed and further refined the concept of the social exchange theory, a theory with roots in economics, psychology, communications, and sociology.
3. We have taken these distinctions from Sportsmind: www.sportsmind .com.
4. Angelo Mazzocco, personal interview, October 2011.
5. Michael Pirson and Deepak Malhotra. "Unconventional Insights for Managing Stakeholder Trust." *Sloan Management Review*, July 1, 2008. (We paraphrased in this section.)
6. Randy York, "Root, Conners Show True Meaning of Team Trust," *Huskers*, November 11, 2011; available at: www.huskers.com/View Article.dbml?DB_OEM_ID=100&ATCLID=205331766.
7. Doug Renfro, personal interview, September 2011.
8. Domonic Biggi, personal interview, October 2011.
9. Jeff Schwantz, personal interview, October 2011.
10. *Ibid.*
11. *Ibid.*

12. Stephen M. R. Covey, *The Speed of Trust: The One Thing That Changes Everything* (New York: Free Press, 2006), p. 15. (We paraphrased in this section.)
13. Jim Hallett, personal interview, September 2011.
14. Bruce Barnes, personal interview, September 2011.
15. Valerie A. Zeithaml, A. Parasuraman, and Leonard L. Berry, *Delivering Quality Service: Balancing Customer Perceptions and Expectations* (New York: Free Press, 1990), pp. 26–28. (We paraphrased in this section.)
16. Domonic Biggi, personal interview, October 2011.
17. *Ibid.*

Key #4: Share Information to Increase Your Personal Power
1. Douglas Southall Freeman, *Lee's Lieutenants: A Study in Command: Cedar Mountain to Chancellorsville*, Vol. 2 (New York: Scribner, 1943), pp. 8–9. (We paraphrased in this section.)
2. *Ibid.*, p. 9.
3. Tom Feeney, personal interview, September 2011.
4. *Ibid.*
5. *Ibid.*
6. *Ibid.*
7. *Ibid.*
8. *Ibid.*
9. James Heskett, *The Culture Cycle: How to Shape the Unseen Force that Transforms Performance* (Upper Saddle River, NJ: Financial Times Press, 2012), p. 2.
10. Jim Hallett, personal interview, September 2011.
11. Tom Feeney, personal interview, September 2011.
12. Derek Smith, personal interview, June 2012.
13. Barry K. Dayton, "Innovation Live: Engaging 3M's Global Employees in Creating an Exciting, Growth-Focused Future," 3M, October 11, 2012; available at: www.managementexchange.com/story/innovationlive-engagin-3ms-global-employees-creating-exciting-growth-focused-future. (We paraphrased in this section.)
14. Don Tapscott and Anthony D. Williams, *Wikinomics: How Mass Collaboration Changes Everything*, expanded edition (New York: Portfolio, 2008), pp. 7–9. (We paraphrased in this section.)
15. *Ibid.*, p. 9.
16. *Ibid.*, p. 10. (We paraphrased in this section.)
17. *Ibid.*, pp. 130–131. (We paraphrased in this section.)

18. Thomas L. Friedman, *The World Is Flat: A Brief History of the Twenty-First Century* (New York: Farrar, Straus & Giroux, 2005), pp. 141–144. (We paraphrased in this section.)
19. James O'Toole and Warren Bennis, "What's Needed Next: A Culture of Candor," *Harvard Business Review*, June 2009, p. 56.

Key #5: Manage Yourself before You Manage Others

1. Robert Burns, "To a Louse: On Seeing One on a Lady's Bonnet, at Church," fragment 8, lines 54–55, 1786; available at: www.robertburns .org/works/97.shtml.
2. Daniel Goleman, *Working with Emotional Intelligence* (New York: Bantam Books, 1998), p. 26.
3. *Ibid.*, p. 52.
4. Bill George, interviewed by David Brancaccio, *Now 311*, PBS, March 16, 2007; available at: www.pbs.org/now/transcript/311.html.
5. Dee Hock, *One from Many: VISA and the Rise of Chaordic Organization* (San Francisco: Barrett-Koehler, 2005), pp. 48–49.
6. Daniel Goleman, *Working with Emotional Intelligence* (New York: Bantam Books, 1998), pp. 33–34.
7. Bill George, "Leadership Starts with Self-Awareness," *Minneapolis Star Tribune*, February 26, 2012.
8. Henry Mintzberg, *Managers Not MBAs: A Hard Look at the Soft Practice of Managing and Management Development* (San Francisco: Barrett-Koehler, 2005), p. 18.
9. *Ibid.*, p. 13.
10. *Ibid.*, pp. 282–283.
11. *Ibid.*, p. 300.
12. *Ibid.*, pp. 301–302.
13. Gary Hamel and C. K. Prahalad, *Competing for the Future: Breakthrough Strategies for Seizing Control of Your Industry and Creating the Markets of Tomorrow* (Boston: Harvard Business School Press, 1994), pp. 4–5.
14. Bill George, *True North: Discover Your Authentic Leadership* (San Francisco: Jossey-Bass, 2007), p. 68.
15. Chris Argyris, "Teaching Smart People How to Learn," *Harvard Business Review*, June 1991.
16. Bill George, *True North: Discover Your Authentic Leadership* (San Francisco: Jossey-Bass, 2007), p. 71.

A Review of the Five Keys

1. Peter E. Rouse, *Every Relationship Matters: Using the Power of Relationships to Transform Your Business, Your Firm, and Yourself* (Chicago: American Bar Association, 2007), p. 24.
2. W. Edwards Deming, *Out of the Crisis* (Cambridge, MA: MIT Press 1986), p. 121.
3. James A. Autry, *Love and Profit: The Art of Caring Leadership* (New York: Avon Books, 1992), p. 46.
4. Maribeth Kuzmeski, *The Connectors: How the World's Most Successful Businesspeople Build Relationships and Win Clients for Life* (Hoboken, NJ: Wiley, 2009), p. xiv. (This book concentrates on sales relationships, and it is an excellent source.)
5. Joan Holmes, personal interview, October 2011.
6. Bruce Barnes, personal interview, September 2011.
7. Joan Holmes, personal interview, October 2011.
8. Doug Renfro, personal interview, September 2011.
9. Nicholas Wolfson, personal interview, October 2011.
10. Domonic Biggi, personal interview, October 2011.

Virtual Relationships and the Five Keys

1. While this quote is omnipresent on the Internet, after six hours of searching, we cannot find the original source. Anyone who does, please send it to us.
2. James Thurber, *Lanterns and Lances* (New York: Harper & Brothers, 1961), p. 41.
3. Alex Ayers, ed., *The Wit and Wisdom of Mark Twain* (New York: Harper Perennial, 2005), p. 252.
4. David Shipley and Will Schwalbe, *Send: The Essential Guide to Email for Office and Home* (New York: Knopf, 2007), pp. 10–11.
5. "Do You Know Your Netiquette?" *Manchester Evening News*, April 27, 2010; available at: www.manchestereveningnews.co.uk/news/uk-news/do-you-know-your-netiquette-1023449.
6. Liz Hull, "Email Etiquette: What Your Response Time Reveals about Your Personality," *Daily Mail*, August 28, 2008; available at: www.dailymail.co.uk/sciencetech/article-1050260/Email-etiquette-What-response-time-reveals-personality.html. (We paraphrased in this section.)

7. Jay Baer, "42 Percent of Consumers Complaining in Social Media Expect 60-Minute Response Time," *Convince and Convert*, September 27, 2012; available at: http://convinceandconvert.com/the-social-habit /42-percent-of-consumers-complaining-in-social-media-expect-60 -minute-response-time.
8. Daniel Goleman, "Flame First, Think Later: New Clues to Email Misbehavior," *New York Times*, February 20, 2007.
9. Zach Bulygo, "What Can You Learn from These 6 Companies that Thrive on Twitter?," Kissmetrics, http://blog.kissmetrics.com/ thrive-on-twitter.
10. *Ibid.*
11. *Ibid.*
12. Devin Dwyer, "Odd Obama Email Subject Lines Drew Huge Cash," *ABC News*, November 29, 2012, http://abcnews.go.com/blogs/ politics/2012/11/odd-obama-email-subject-lines-drew-huge-cash. (We paraphrased in this section.)
13. Joshua Green, "The Science Behind Those Obama Campaign E-mails," *Bloomberg Business Week*, November 29, 2012; available at: www .businessweek.com/articles/2012-11-29/the-science-behind-those -obama-campaign-e-mails. (We paraphrased in this section.)
14. Charles Newkey-Burden, *Great Email Disasters* (London: Metro Publishing, 2007), p. 39.
15. *Ibid.*, pp. 39–41. (We paraphrased in this section.)
16. Alicia Androich, "Rogers' Very Bad Twitter Day," *Marketing*, March 19, 2012; available at: www.marketingmag.ca/news/media-news/ rogers-very-bad-twitter-day-48841.
17. Zach Bulygo, "What Can You Learn from These 6 Companies that Thrive on Twitter?," Kissmetrics, http://blog.kissmetrics.com/ thrive-on-twitter.
18. We have taken these distinctions from Sportsmind: www.sportsmind .com.
19. Brad Stone and Noam Cohen, "Social Networks Spread Defiance Online," *New York Times*, June 15, 2009; available at: www.nytimes.com/ 2009/06/16/world/middleeast/16media.html.
20. "Social Media's Role in Egyptian, Arab World Protests," PBS, February 15, 2011; available at: www.pbs.org/newshour/extra/video/ blog/2011/02/social_medias_role_in_egyptian.html.
21. Joan Holmes, personal interview, October 2011.
22. Facebook entry most easily accessed at: www.facebook.com/ GotWhatItCakes.

23. Steve Hall, "Ford Slaps Brand Enthusiasts, Returns Love with Legal Punch," Adrants, January 14, 2008; available at: www.adrants.com/2008/01/ford-slaps-brand-enthusiasts-returns.php.

24. Tom Peters, *Liberation Management: Necessary Disorganization for the Nanosecond Nineties* (New York: Knopf, 1992), p. 722.

For Leaders: Three Relationship Challenges

1. John P. Kotter, "What Leaders Really Do." *Harvard Business Review*, December 2001, p. 86.

2. Julia Boorstin, "The Best Advice I Ever Got: Warren Buffett, Richard Branson, Meg Whitman, A. G. Lafley, and 24 Other Luminaries on the People Who Most Influenced Their Lives." *Fortune*, March 21, 2005, p. 100.

3. Bill George, *True North: Discover Your Authentic Leadership* (San Francisco: Jossey-Bass, 2007), p. 18.

4. *Ibid.*, pp. 3–4.

5. Bill George, Peter Sims, Andrew N. McLean, and Diana Mayer, "Discovering Your Authentic Leadership," *Harvard Business Review*, February 2007; available at: http://hbr.org/2007/02/discovering-your-authentic-leadership/ar/1.

6. Harry M. Jansen Kraemer, Jr., "The Only True Leadership Is Value-Based Leadership," *Forbes*, April 26, 2011; available at: www.forbes.com/2011/04/26/values-based-leadership.html. (We paraphrased in this section.)

7. Jerry MacArthur Hultin, personal interview, October 2011.

8. Dee Hock, *One from Many: VISA and the Rise of Chaordic Organization* (San Francisco: Barrett-Koehler, 2005), pp. 21–23. (Our emphasis and we paraphrased in this section.)

9. James Heskett, *The Culture Cycle: How to Shape the Unseen Force that Transforms Performance* (Upper Saddle River, NJ: Financial Times Press, 2012), p. 2.

10. *Ibid.*, p. 7.

11. The concepts of *wicked* and *tame* problems refers to problems that are difficult or impossible to solve. See Wikipedia at http://wikipedia.org/wiki/wicked-problem for further references regarding this topic.

Index

About the Authors

For almost three decades Sallie J. Sherman, Joseph P. Sperry and, more recently, Steve Vucelich have been helping companies increase revenues, reduce costs, and lower risk by helping firms optimize their B2B relationships so those companies can grow and thrive.

Sallie J. Sherman, PhD, is an expert in helping businesses grow by transforming their B2B relationships into strategic assets. Since 1986, she has been focusing on auditing clients' key relationships—both internally and externally—and then using that information to collaboratively help companies design and execute relationship management strategies that create a sustainable, competitive advantage. As a result, she also helps companies improve their B2B customer experience and be more customer-driven. In addition, she advises clients on relationship recovery issues and serves as a trusted advisor to C-suite leaders on a variety of other internal and external relationship issues. Sallie is the founder and CEO of S4 Consulting and coauthor of *The Seven Keys to Strategic Account Management*.

Joseph P. Sperry, PhD is a recognized authority on the principles and application of relationship management programs. Joe has written and lectured for more than 25 years on customer loyalty, service and relationship quality, and strategic relationship development. Through thousands of Fortune 500 interviews of critical account relationships, he has developed and delivered countless programs on how to make relationship management programs a strategic advantage. Joe is a retired partner at S4 Consulting and coauthor of *The Seven Keys to Strategic Account Management*.

Steve Vucelich specializes in helping companies assess customer relationships, design and implement relationship management programs, and unleash customer profitability. His experience in competitive intelligence and financial analysis helps clients increase the profitability of their critical business relationships. As a result of his work, clients across a range of industries are better able to identify additional profitable business opportunities and to evaluate innovative approaches to partnering with customers. Steve Vucelich is vice president and partner at S4 Consulting and is a frequently requested speaker.

Ready to put the keys into action?

Learn how to unlock the potential of business relationships to boost individual influence and organizational success using our FREE, easy-to-understand printable worksheet available online.

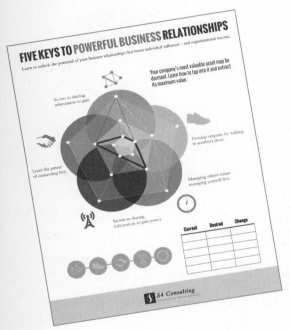

- Learn how to spot the relationships that are not generating their full power—and turn them into drivers of profit and growth.

- Discover new ways to eliminate barriers to performance and boost the energy of individuals, teams, groups, and your organization as a whole.

- Find out how to improve personal and managerial development by using *Five Keys to Powerful Business Relationships*.

Grab your **complimentary tool** to help you better manage business relationships online at

FIVEKEYSBOOK.COM